natural
health
for kids

Sarah Wilson

natural health for kids

Self-help and complementary treatments for more than 100 ailments

hamlyn

First published in Great Britain in 2006 by Hamlyn,
a division of Octopus Publishing Group Ltd
2–4 Heron Quays, London E14 4JP

Distributed in the United States and Canada by
Sterling Publishing Co., Inc.
387 Park Avenue South, New York, NY 10016–8810

ISBN 0 600 61355 0
EAN 9780600613558

The moral right of the author has been asserted.

A CIP catalogue record for this book is available
from the British Library

Printed and bound in China

10 9 8 7 6 5 4 3 2 1

**This book is not intended as an alternative to
personal medical advice. The reader should consult
a physician in all matters relating to health and
particularly in respect of any symptoms which may
require diagnosis or medical attention. While the
advice and information are believed to be accurate
and true at the time of going to press, neither the
author nor the publisher can accept any legal
responsibility or liability for any errors or
omissions that may have been made.**

contents

the holistic approach to health

Every parent wants to have a healthy child. Yet children today weigh more and are less fit than ever before. They eat more junk food, take less exercise, are ferried around in cars, and spend hours slumped in front of TVs and computers, all of which combine to have a huge impact on their health. Indeed, experts are warning of a crisis due to this dangerous combination of a sedentary modern lifestyle and unhealthy diet.

Maybe you are reading this book because you have already started to see the effects of this on your own child. Maybe he has a permanent runny nose, gets one infection after another or is often under the weather. You may have already reached the conclusion that antibiotics are not the answer, as they seem to lower your child's immunity in the long run.

The sticking-plaster approach seems to be endemic. Rather than looking at the underlying causes of ill health and ways of preventing it, we have instead become dependent on drugs and surgical procedures as the answer to everything. However, as more and more bugs are becoming resistant to antibiotics, we need to find new, long-term solutions.

All many childhood illnesses really need is a back-to-basics approach – some simple tender loving care, rest and relaxation – and time to mend. This is where this book comes in, as a helpful tool for parents everywhere.

the conventional approach

Conventional medical approaches are based on detailed scientific knowledge and academic research, and have a great track record in diagnosing disease. The emphasis is on fighting and destroying disease through the use of drugs and surgery, focusing on the symptoms rather than the cause.

Doctors tend to specialize in a chosen field, so they do not view the patient as a whole. The key determining factor is the assumption that everyone is the same, and this is the key principle dominating trials in conventional medicine. While this was good enough for many people in the previous century, there are now signs of an increasing disenchantment with conventional medicine. One of the biggest problems is that the side-effects of modern drugs can be so debilitating. Unfortunately, many of the treatments that doctors prescribe deal only with the symptoms of the complaint, rather than addressing the root cause of the problem itself.

Modern medicine has achieved a great deal, but it also has a lot to answer for, and more and more people are seeking an alternative way. Doctors themselves are becoming more aware of the benefits of complementary health therapies when conventional medicine does not seem to be working, and the integrated approach is gaining more and more support. A study at the University of Sheffield in 2001 showed that 49 per cent of doctors in England gave patients access to complementary therapy. It seems that what people want is choice.

However, it is important to remember that conventional medicine saves lives when it comes to serious conditions such as cancer, cardiovascular disease and diabetes, whereas complementary medicine can play a supporting role but not cure, for instance by helping to alleviate the associated stress and anxiety, and improving quality of life.

the complementary approach

Once regarded as eccentric and on the fringes, complementary medicine is now viewed as acceptable, and more and more people are putting their faith in their own experiences rather than in the cold facts of conventional medical research. Statistics show that a quarter of us have now tried complementary therapies and that one in ten people consult a complementary therapist before visiting their doctor, irrespective of the nature of their complaint. Some therapies, such as homeopathy, osteopathy and chiropractic, are now even seen as mainstream.

Complementary medicine is based on holistic principles, with the person being treated as a whole. It is a very humane process, based on touch, communication and relating to people, instead of reaching automatically for a prescription pad. Therapists build up a complete picture of an individual's case by asking detailed questions about lifestyle, diet, exercise, medical history and general health. The idea is that, if people are involved in their own health care and the advice makes sense to them, the outcome of treatment is likely to be much better. The emphasis is on strengthening the body's immune system and looking at the root cause of the problem and how it can be addressed. Many therapists believe that drugs add to the body's toxic load and that surgery really is the last resort.

why the natural approach is good for children

As parents you want the best for your child – and for many of you the natural approach may instinctively seem the best way to go. Complementary therapies are gentle and holistic, and will boost your child's immune system so that it can start healing itself naturally. This belief that the body has an inherent ability to heal itself is fundamental to natural health. Holistic therapies help parents to build a caring and healthy relationship with their children, in which they start listening to their bodies rather than showering them with quick-fix solutions.

With conventional medicine, the symptoms of illness are suppressed by drugs, and the immune system is not given the opportunity it needs to kick in and activate your body's own healing processes. A child's immune system is a delicate thing, and a constant onslaught of antibiotics, steroids and other invasive drugs can weaken it, putting your child into a constant loop of illness. An efficient immune system is the key to a healthy child. It helps to fight infection and allergies, and will enable your child to get the most out of life without being hindered by illness.

Complementary medicine represents a more subtle approach to health. For example, if your child has tonsillitis and you take him to see your doctor, the doctor will prescribe penicillin – and the same will happen for every other child with tonsillitis across the length and breadth of the country. Yet the way that illness manifests itself is not the same for all children, and it is essential to look at the complete picture, taking into account factors such as lifestyle, nutrition and emotional aspects. This is where complementary medicine comes into its own.

nutrition

The whole question of what children eat has never been more topical. It is not easy to keep your children on the right track, and you will face many challenges. Advertising, peer pressure, the need for convenience, and addiction to sugar all affect your children's eating habits. This is a big issue and there is no easy solution. But by establishing healthy nutritional building blocks you can at least set your child on the right path.

The average diet of children in many wealthy, industrialized countries is not good. Fed on a high-sugar, high-fat, high-salt combination, with all sorts of additives thrown in for good measure, our children are at risk of behavioural problems and long-term health issues. You can often keep control of things in the pre-school years, when a party bag once a month is usually your biggest challenge, but once a child walks through the school gates it's a jungle. You also have to keep things in perspective, because you cannot possibly control everything. It's best to aim for moderation and 'cut them some slack' with the occasional treat.

Your aim should be threefold: good nutrition will help your child to maintain a healthy weight, provides fuel for learning activities and physical exercise, and will help her to learn the right food choices that will serve her throughout her life.

Sources of mineral nutrients

Here are some child-friendly sources of essential minerals:

Iron pumpkin seeds, prunes, cashew nuts and raisins

Calcium cheese and dairy products

Folate wheatgerm, spinach, sesame seeds and broccoli

Zinc lamb, haddock, split peas, peas, egg yolks and oats

the foundations of a healthy diet

• First sit down and review your whole family's eating habits to see what sort of messages you are sending out. If meals are rushed affairs and you tend not to sit down together as a family, perhaps you should start setting aside time in your busy day to give meals more priority.

• Aim for a 'balanced plate' approach to nutrition. Unless your child has any food intolerances (see page 112), a healthy diet consists of the right mixture of complex carbohydrates (rice, pasta and bread), dairy products (milk, yogurt and cheese), protein (meat, fish, eggs and pulses), and plenty of fresh fruit and vegetables.

• Research shows that breakfast really is the most important meal of the day. Yet statistics reveal that one in five children miss breakfast altogether, going to school on an empty stomach. Children who eat breakfast are less likely to be over-weight and more likely to perform better and have fewer behavioural problems than those who skip it.

• Always read the labels on food packaging – and look out for hidden salt, sugar and fats in basic foods, such as breakfast cereals, biscuits, bread and cereal bars. Wherever possible, you should give your child a pure, natural diet of foods that are free from artificial colourings, flavouring and preservatives.

exercise

In our car-obsessed, TV-reliant society, most children simply do not get enough exercise, and this is a major health concern for parents. Toddlers love to move around and are very active, running and climbing at every opportunity. However, as they grow older, children can slow down in the face of the increasing demands made on them by school.

encouraging your child to exercise

• Encourage your child to be active wherever possible. In this way, she will develop stronger muscles and bones, and a leaner body. She will therefore be less likely to carry excess weight, which is a key factor in the development of serious diseases such as diabetes.

• Provide plenty of opportunities for exercise. If possible, start thinking about walking to school or nursery. If your child does not like more structured sports classes, such as swimming or tennis, take a ball to the park, play hide-and-seek or chasing games – whatever it takes to get everyone moving.

• Treat exercise as fun, not another chore. Praise your child for making an effort, which will boost her self-confidence, and as a result make her enjoy physical activity even more.

• Help your child learn how to cope with the stresses and anxiety of everyday life with exercises such as yoga. This can boost fitness, build confidence, help concentration and balance your child's emotions.

• Good sports for children include walking, running, swimming and dancing, and ball sports, such as football and tennis, which improve coordination skills.

sleep

Children generally need 10–12 hours sleep a night – but that is not to say that they get it! There are many factors to take into account if your child is experiencing disturbed sleep patterns. Illness aside, one of the main factors is stress within the family or at school, which can lead to feelings of insecurity. Children can get over-tired, which can itself lead to sleep problems, and lack of exercise and fresh air is also a contributory factor. Your child may be eating more to compensate for lack of energy, and will be grumpy and irritable.

the foundations of good sleep

• First try to work out what is causing your child's sleep problem. Talk to your child to find out whether anything is troubling him. Take a fresh look at his bedroom – is it too hot and stuffy? It should be cool, dark and quiet.

• Cut out junk foods from your child's diet, especially those containing sugar or caffeine, as these can give children an energy 'rush' that can lead to sleep problems.

• Limit TV before bedtime – an over-stimulated mind means that your child will find it harder to relax into sleep mode.

• Do not let your child eat, work or watch TV in bed – all these activities will leave his mind racing.

• Aim for a balance between work and play in your child's life, as too much of either can disrupt his sleep patterns.

• Taking regular exercise can really help – lack of exercise will make your child feel lethargic because just lying or sitting does not boost his circulation.

• Your child's body clock craves consistency. Always make sleep a priority and put it before distractions such as an extra bedtime story. Get him into a routine of going to bed and getting up at the same time every day.

• Encourage your child to wind down and relax before bedtime. Relaxation techniques can really help.

taking precautions

There are several emergency situations where it is vital to go directly to hospital, or at least phone your doctor if you are in any doubt about your child's health.

when to call the doctor

If you are worried about your child, always call your doctor to set your mind at rest. Outside of surgery hours, take your child to the accident and emergency department of the nearest hospital.

call an ambulance if your child is suffering from any of the following:

- Unconsciousness
- Severe bleeding
- Choking
- A neck or head injury
- Suspected poisoning

Safety in the sun

Take great care of your child whenever he is exposed to the sun, especially in hot climates. Make sure that he has adequate protection by dressing him appropriately and using a sunscreen. Keep him out of direct sunlight during the hottest part of the day.

contact your doctor immediately if your child is suffering from any of the following:

- Severe breathlessness
- An allergic reaction with facial swelling
- Sensitivity to light, with a stiff neck and a rash that remains when a glass is pressed against the skin
- Repeated vomiting and diarrhoea
- A temperature of more than 39°C (102°F) that is not responding to paracetamol
- Unexplained drowsiness or listlessness
- Severe abdominal pain
- Convulsions

go to a hospital emergency department if your child has:

- A suspected fracture
- A cut that needs stitches
- An injury to the eye

complementary therapies

introduction

There is a range of complementary remedies that can enhance your child's health and well-being, and successfully treat a variety of conditions, providing safer alternatives to conventional medicines, such as antibiotics and steroids.

The approach is a gentle one that encourages patients to participate in their own recovery. Holistic practitioners focus on the underlying cause of a disease rather than its symptoms. They work closely with the individual on a long-term basis to help achieve a healthy balance between body, mind and spirit, which is known as homeostasis. Because no two people are alike, great emphasis is placed on the uniqueness of the individual. The therapies that have been chosen here are particularly beneficial to children and are grouped into appropriate categories.

contents

diagnostic therapies

iridology

For a long time, the eyes have been thought to reveal a lot about our health. Iridology is a therapy that examines the iris in order to get a better picture of what is happening in the body as a whole, as many signs of ill health register in the eyes. A key factor is that iridology is a preventive medicine, and can reveal a lot about tendencies to ill health.

uses of iridology

Iridology is suitable for people of all ages. It is a preventive therapy and, as such, can detect problems that may lead to illness. For example, a child who is the blue-eyed 'lymphatic type' (see box) has an inherent tendency to irritations of the adenoids and tonsils, swollen lymph nodes, catarrh, eczema, asthma, coughs, bronchitis, sinusitis, diarrhoea and eye irritations.

the first treatment

The first visit usually lasts about an hour. The iridologist will ask you to fill in a questionnaire about your child's lifestyle, medical history, diet and general health, which he will use when deciding on treatment. First he will first examine the colour and markings of the iris. Then he will look into your child's eyes with a torch and a magnifying glass. He may also take a photograph of your child's eye to view in detail on a large screen. Both methods are non-invasive and will not cause any pain or distress.

The iridologist will then assess the information that he has gathered. Spots of colour, the pattern of fibres and the position of marks on the eye are all relevant. He will look at a detailed chart, showing how each part of the eye relates to a particular area of the body, in order to further identify any problems.

This will provide the vital information needed to establish the root cause of your child's illness, from which the iridologist can work out the best treatment and provide guidance on ways of reversing existing conditions.

how does iridology work?

Iridology concerns the study of the iris – the coloured part of the eye, which consists of nerve endings, each nerve being connected to the brain. An iridologist sees these nerve endings as a 'map' that reveals information about the body's genetic strengths and weaknesses and how effectively the body is functioning at any time.

Iridology is a safe, non-invasive diagnostic therapy that can be integrated into both conventional and complementary medicine. It can help your child learn about his strengths and weaknesses, and to become aware of how he can help himself.

Research studies

Medical research in several European countries has led to a greater acceptance of iridology. A trial in Russia showed diagnosis by iridology to be 85 per cent accurate, while in South Korea clinical trials by the government found that diagnosis was 78.2 per cent accurate on average but 90.2 per cent accurate in the case of digestive disorders.

Constitutional groupings in iridology

In iridology, there are three distinct constitutions:

• Blue-eyed – known as the **lymphatic type**

• Brown-eyed – known as the **haematogenic type**

• A combination of the two – known as the **mixed type** or **biliary type**.

kinesiology

Kinesiology is a holistic system of natural health care that combines modern methods of muscle-testing and energy-balancing with traditional complementary therapies, such as traditional Chinese medicine, acupuncture, chiropractic, nutrition, herbalism and homeopathy.

It uses simple, safe, precise muscle-testing procedures to pinpoint any problem areas, and massage, touch, nutrition, energy reflexes and counselling to rebalance the mind–body connection so that it functions in a healthier way. It also offers a variety of self-help techniques that can be particularly useful when working with children.

uses of kinesiology

Everyone from newborn babies to the elderly can benefit from kinesiology. If your child cannot be tested directly because he is too young, the test can be done with you holding your child as a 'surrogate'. It is helpful in dealing with a range of common childhood complaints, such as allergies, asthma, eczema, recurrent ear, nose and throat infections, food intolerances, sleep disorders, behavioural problems and dyslexia. It can effectively deal with issues such as low energy levels, depleted immune system and poor nutrition. It can also help with mental problems, including lack of concentration, poor memory, lack of motivation, hyperactivity and the now increasingly prevalent attention deficit and hyperactivity disorder (ADHD).

Using a combination of massage, nutrition and other simple techniques, kinesiology can help with emotions and anxieties and energy blocks. It is a therapy that balances the whole person and enhances health and well-being. It can also play a preventive role in warding off disease.

You do not have to be ill to benefit from kinesiology. Even when there is no obvious problem, it may be possible to improve health, well-being, physical or intellectual functioning, attitude or potential. It can help your child to achieve his true potential in sport and to pass examinations. Regular sessions can also keep stress levels under control.

the first treatment

Kinesiologists often specialize in one particular field, such as applied or health kinesiology. Alternatively, they may combine kinesiology with another therapy, such as osteopathy or nutrition.

The kinesiologist will first question you about your child's health and lifestyle, take notes on his diet and observe his posture. Then she will ask your child to lie on the treatment couch so that she can test his muscles by applying light pressure to specific areas of his body. For example, she may ask your child to raise one arm and, on the instruction to 'hold', to try to match her light pressure for a couple of seconds. If your child is unable to respond, she might massage or touch a point on his body or head to strengthen a muscle, so that the flow of energy through the body is revitalized.

Your child should find this an enjoyable and relaxing experience, and there is nothing to worry about. In a single session, the kinesiologist may identify allergies, make nutritional recommendations, deal with phobias and stress, and rebalance the body's energy.

No two sessions of treatment are the same, even for children with similar symptoms, because every individual is treated as unique. This holistic approach of addressing both physical and psychological issues makes it an especially powerful healing system, which is being recognized increasingly by members of the medical profession.

how does kinesiology work?

The word 'kinesiology' comes from the Greek word *kinesis*, meaning 'motion'. It is a touch-based therapy that uses gentle muscle-testing to evaluate body function. It involves applying light pressure to a muscle and monitoring the response. Once the stresses have been identified, gentle techniques are used to bring the body back into harmony with itself.

applied kinesiology

This is a diagnostic therapy that works on the link between the muscles and the meridians, or energy pathways, of the acupuncture system. The kinesiologist uses a series of basic manual muscle tests to assess problem areas. A strong muscle response indicates a balanced state while a weak muscle response indicates a problem.

Once a problem has been located, she applies an appropriate correction to change the response to a strong one. Corrections include massage or light touch on specific reflex points, energizing acupuncture points, emotional balancing, muscle activation and nutritional support. Stimulation of reflex points on the body can instantly strengthen weak muscles and improve posture and body function.

Primarily concerned with muscle function, applied kinesiology works on the principle that the body is a self-maintaining, self-correcting mechanism. Many basic treatment methods in osteopathy, chiropractic, acupuncture and homeopathy produce an immediate improvement in muscular function, and these can be directly measured by manual muscle-testing. This type of testing does not diagnose disease but can detect minor functional imbalances. These can accumulate and cause symptoms of discomfort, pain or even allergic reactions. If these warnings are ignored, poor health can result.

health kinesiology

This focuses on allergies, weight loss and stress. It is a gentle system of healing, suitable for people of all ages and dispositions, including children and babies. Common forms of treatment include homeopathic remedies, flower essences, or even concentrating on a particular thought. Most children find the session a relaxing and enjoyable experience, and feel much better afterwards.

natural therapies

aromatherapy

One of the most popular and best-known complementary therapies, aromatherapy can be a powerful treatment. The benefits of using essential oils is now widely recognized and is being used increasingly as part of an integrated approach to treating illness, with essential oils being used alongside more conventional methods. Children of all ages can benefit from aromatherapy and love the idea of healing through the power of smell. They also respond very well to massage.

uses of aromatherapy

Aromatherapy can help a range of conditions, ranging from skin complaints, such as eczema, to stress-related problems, such as insomnia and anxiety. It can be used to help your child get well or to give them a general lift in terms of well-being. It also plays a role in terms of preventive medicine, as it can boost the immune system and counteract the negative effects of stress. Essential oils can help with physical conditions and health issues ranging from asthma to attention deficit and hyperactivity disorder (ADHD).

Essential oils are now widely available in pharmacies, supermarkets and health-food shops. Be sure to buy a reputable brand rather than a cheaper blend. It is important to use only oils that are safe for babies and children, such as rose, lavender and chamomile, and always to use them in the right dosage. If in doubt, always consult a qualified practitioner.

How to use essential oils

There are various ways of using essential oils.

• Add them to body oils, lotions, creams and gels and apply them directly to your child's skin.

• Add them to water, for example to your child's bath or shower, or use them as a compress or as a rinse to sponge down your child.

• Diffuse them into the air via a vaporizer, burner or spray, so that your child inhales them.

• Add a few drops to a bowl of water or a tissue so that your child can inhale them.

Store essential oils in a cool, dark place. Use within a year of opening as the oils start to deteriorate and lose their strength once exposed to air.

the first treatment

The aromatherapist will take a detailed case history of your child in order to get a full picture of her current state of health and to note any previous problems. He will also take into account any emotional worries that may be causing stress, or other psychological issues that may be triggering symptoms of illness. Once the therapist has a complete picture, he will decide which essential oils are best suited to treating your child and how best to use them.

Although you may want to treat your child yourself, it is always best to consult a trained practitioner first, especially where children are concerned. You will then be in the best possible position to continue treating your child at home.

how does aromatherapy work?

Aromatherapy is holistic in its approach, the idea being that essential oils affect the mind as well as the body. Moreover, one of its guiding principles is the strong connection between touch, through massage, and a sense of well-being.

Therapists use about 60 oils or plant essences, which are distilled from flowers, leaves, seeds, herbs, bark, resin and roots. They are 100 per cent pure and natural. The body absorbs the essential oils and eliminates them rapidly.

Essential oils are complex substances that work in harmony with the body and can have far-reaching effects. Each essential oil has its own particular healing property. Lavender, for example, has a gentle, sedative effect and is often used to help those with sleeping problems. Rosemary, on the other hand, is stimulating. Other oils have antiseptic (thyme linalol), anti-bacterial (tea tree), anti-inflammatory (Roman and German chamomile) or anti-spasmodic (cardamom) properties.

Combining essential oils gives greater flexibility. While a single oil has certain properties of its own, mixing two oils together creates a combination that is able to help another set of conditions.

The oils work on the body in two different ways:
- Physiologically, where they work on the actual physical condition of the patient.
- Psychologically, where they work via the sense of smell and the effect they have on the mind.

Precautions when using essential oils

Essential oils are powerful, highly concentrated substances and should always be used in moderation – sometimes it is quite usual to use just a single drop. They must be diluted with a carrier oil, such as grape-seed oil, before they are applied to the skin.

The usual recommended dilution for children is 3–5 drops of essential oil to every 2 tablespoonsful of carrier oil, although this depends on the age of the child. For children under 6 years old, no more than 2 drops of essential oil per 2 tablespoonsful of base oil should be used for massage, in the bath or in a vaporizer.

Some oils may be toxic if they are not used correctly. Other oils, such as bergamot, neroli and citrus, can cause irritation if the skin is exposed to sunlight after their use. All essential oils should be kept out of reach of children.

Research studies

Research in Germany has shown that peppermint and eucalyptus oils may reduce the pain associated with headaches: applying the oils with a sponge to the forehead and temples reduced the pain in over 50 per cent of cases. In the USA, researchers are carrying out a study to see if some smells can help weight-loss.

homeopathy

Homeopathy is one of the fastest-growing complementary therapies and one of the most widely accepted. In France, for example, seven out of ten doctors claim to prescribe homeopathic remedies at least occasionally.

The homeopathic approach is holistic, based on the principle of treating the whole person, not just the symptoms. So, two people with the same condition may be given different remedies because they have different characteristics and therefore different needs. It is also preventive, helping to maintain health by boosting the immune system and warding off any potential illness. This very gentle therapy works by stimulating the energy system, which encourages the body to heal naturally.

uses of homeopathy

Homeopathy can help with a wide range of both physical and emotional childhood conditions, ranging from bed-wetting, bad behaviour and bruises to influenza and tonsillitis. It can also act as a support to conventional medical treatment. Children tend to like homeopathic remedies because the medicines taste pleasant. Also, they respond more quickly to treatment than adults because they have higher levels of energy.

Certain conditions can be treated at home since a number of common remedies are available from pharmacies and health-food stores. However, you should always seek the advice of a qualified homeopath before attempting any home treatment. A good place to start is by observing your child carefully and taking notes in order to build up a case history. This will include everything from basics, such as taking his temperature and assessing whether he is thirstier than usual, to examining his tongue and recording his food aversions. You can then use this infomation to decide on an appropriate remedy.

the first treatment

The initial consultation usually takes about an hour, during which the homeopath will take a detailed history of your child's health and lifestyle. This will cover any medical problems – such as past illnesses or operations, and any drugs or medication that could have suppressed symptoms – as well as environmental factors, diet, exercise, sleep patterns and personality.

The homeopath will also take a detailed family history, looking at genetic factors and any predisposition to disease. She may even ask you, as the mother, about the pregnancy and birth, and if there were any stressful circumstances surrounding them. She will also need to know about any issues that may have caused upheaval in your child's life, such as moving house or the birth of a sibling. Finally, she will look at your child's posture, hair and skin tone.

Once she has a complete picture, the homeopath will prescribe treatment. This usually includes advice on nutrition, exercise and other lifestyle factors, as well as the homeopathic remedy itself. This is known as 'constitutional treatment'.

how does homeopathy work?

Homeopathy is based on the belief that the body has the capacity to heal itself as long as it is in balance, but loss of this balance results in illness. It works on the principle that 'like cures like' and involves the prescription of minute doses of substances that produce symptoms similar to those of the illness in order to kick-start your body's own healing processes. For example, if you are stung by a bee you will experience stinging pain and your skin will redden. Yet Apis, which is made from bee venom, is one of the best remedies for insect bites. The homeopath takes all aspects of the child into account, looking at symptoms on every level – mental, emotional and physical – and building up a complete picture in order to treat him.

Another fundamental principle of homeopathy is that no two individuals are the same and each case needs to be looked at separately because the symptoms are unique to that particular person. As a result, the homeopath will prescribe specific remedies appropriate to the symptoms and personal situation of the individual.

Homeopathic remedies are based mainly on plant, mineral or animal substances, and are given in a diluted form. They are prepared by dissolving the substance in a solvent, such as alcohol, then diluting it many times. Strange as it may seem, the greater the number of dilutions, the more powerful the remedy. Remedies usually take the form of pills or granules, which are dissolved on the tongue (granules are particularly suitable for children), or tinctures, which are mixed with water. Ointments, creams and powders are also available.

Unlike conventional drugs, which suppress the immune system, homeopathic medicine is supportive, allowing your child's body to start healing itself. Your child will need to avoid peppermint in all forms (including toothpaste – you will need to buy a homeopathic brand), as it will compromise the effectiveness of the remedies. Some prescription drugs may also interfere with homeopathic remedies, so always tell your homeopath if your child is taking any other medication.

Research studies

Trials have shown a significant reduction in the symptoms of acute childhood diarrhoea after homeopathic treatment, while other studies have found homoeopathy useful in the treatment of hay fever, influenza, pain, sprains and upper respiratory tract infections.

Warning Always consult a qualified homeopath. All medicines, even homeopathic ones, should be stored securely in case your child mistakes them for sweets.

nutritional therapy

When it comes to what children eat, good nutrition and a healthy balanced diet are now seen as vital to maintaining good health and protecting against disease. Poor nutrition affects their health both now and in the future, and can eventually lead to heart disease, weight problems, cancer and diabetes. Many childhood complaints, such as allergies, asthma, ear infections, constipation and skin conditions, have a direct link with diet. The right foods power up your child's immune system, while the wrong foods can weaken it and leave her vulnerable to infection. The nutritional approach to maintaining good health is gathering momentum.

In most developed countries, there is a trend now towards a high-fat, high-sugar diet that results in children piling on extra kilos, developing food intolerances and becoming ill from diseases such as diabetes. As a result, children weigh more and are less fit than ever before, and this generation is the heaviest ever recorded. According to the latest UK government figures, obesity levels in children have risen by a staggering 50 per cent in just seven years, with over 15 per cent of children aged under 11 years now classed as obese.

Not only are today's children fat but they are also often malnourished. When it comes to deficiencies, studies show that iron, calcium, folate and zinc are the main nutrients missing from children's diet.

uses of nutritional therapy

Nutritional therapy is suitable for everyone, and everyone can learn from it. It plays an important role in the prevention and treatment of serious conditions, such as cancer and heart disease, and in the diagnosis and treatment of common childhood ailments, such as eczema and asthma. For example, many asthmatic children benefit from the elimination of dairy products from their diet. There is also a link between recurrent ear infections and sensitivity to cow's milk. Many children have difficulty digesting milk or, more specifically, the lactose in milk, which passes into the large intestine in an undigested state, causing cramps, bloating and diarrhoea.

According to a Belgian study, vitamin B2 (riboflavin) can reduce the frequency of headaches when taken as a preventive medicine. Vitamin B2 is found in wholegrains, eggs, green leafy vegetables and dairy products.

Warning Always seek professional advice before eliminating any food from your child's diet.

the first treatment

The nutritionist will first take a full history of your child's daily food intake, so it helps to keep a food diary for a week or two before the appointment. He will also build up a picture of your child by asking about her past and present medical history, including any current symptoms, known allergies or intolerances, plus questions relating to her lifestyle in general. He may also carry out some simple tests in order to eliminate any possible allergies and food intolerances, and to see if she has any nutritional deficiencies.

Treatment usually involves a diet sheet tailored to your individual child. Once the nutritionist has pinpointed any foods that trigger a reaction, he may suggest a rotation diet, in which the food is not banned entirely but is not eaten every day. The idea behind this is that the body can become over-sensitized to a certain food if it has to deal with it on a daily basis. This may work in some cases, but other children may have to eliminate the food from their diet completely.

You will be able to 'treat' your child at home. Taking your nutritionist's advice into account, you should make any necessary adjustments, aiming for a 'balanced plate' approach to nutrition. As stated in the Introduction (see Nutrition, page 8), when it comes to good nutrition, you should aim to maintain her weight at a healthy level, provide her with fuel for learning and physical activity, and encourage her to choose the right foods.

With allowances for food allergies, a healthy diet consists of the right mixture of complex carbohydrates (rice, pasta and bread), dairy products (milk, yogurt and cheese), protein (meat, fish, eggs, pulses) and plenty of fresh fruit and vegetables (see also Nutrition, page 8). Always read the labels, looking out for hidden salt, sugar, fats and additives. The best way to ensure that your child gets the key nutrients to maintain and promote good health is to give her good-quality fresh foods and to ban junk foods from her diet.

how does nutritional therapy work?

Based on the principle that the vital elements in food can help the healing process, a healthy diet is a preventive tool. Under certain circumstances, some foods are responsible for causing disease and illness. The idea is to improve and maintain your child's health through what she eats. In some cases, and depending on what tests reveal, you may need to eliminate certain foods from her diet completely if they are causing health problems.

Children are increasingly affected by allergies and food intolerances. The most common allergens are milk, wheat, peanuts, eggs, fish and soya, although almost any food can trigger symptoms in certain children. When a child has a food allergy, her body treats the food as a foreign substance, triggering an allergic reaction that can affect the skin, respiratory system and stomach. Symptoms can range in severity from a mild case of hives to a life-threatening anaphylactic reaction. Food allergies involve an over-reaction of the immune system to the food, causing symptoms such as bloating, headaches, hives and diarrhoea.

The chances of your child having a food allergy are increased if she is exposed to allergenic foods as a baby, or if there is a parent or sibling with a food allergy. In the UK, it is estimated that 1–2 per cent of children suffer from food allergy. A national poll in the USA found recently that 10 per cent of allergies were triggered by food. Food sensitivities, also known as food intolerances, are less serious than allergy.

Nutritional therapy and special diets

Your child may just be a fussy eater, in which case she could be deficient in certain nutrients and you might consider giving her a nutritional supplement.

If your child is vegetarian, make sure that she eats plenty of beans, lentils and other pulses and is not over-reliant on dairy foods. Studies by the American Dietetic Association show that vegetarian children have a higher IQ.

If your child is vegan, her plant-based diet means that she will have a healthier heart, less likelihood of weight problems and a lower risk of diabetes.

naturopathy

Naturopathy is a complete system of natural health care based on the belief that the body has the capacity to heal itself and that the secret of good health lies in the healing powers of nature. Symptoms are viewed as the body's attempt to heal itself and treatment addresses the underlying causes of illness, which usually stem from a poor quality of lifestyle. Naturopathy is very much an 'umbrella' therapy and includes a range of complementary therapies, including homeopathy, nutritional therapy, acupuncture and herbalism.

The principles of naturopathy

There are three basic principles of naturopathy:

• The body has the wisdom and power to heal itself, and treatment should enhance this.

• The body has a natural drive to maintain equilibrium, and symptoms of disease are seen as indications that the body is trying to heal itself.

• The root cause of all disease is the accumulation of waste products and toxins due to poor lifestyle.

uses of naturopathy

Gentle and effective, naturopathy is particularly suitable for children and can be used to treat a wide variety of complaints. At a time when modern technology, environmental pollution, bad eating habits and stress are together having a huge impact on children's health, the naturopath uses natural therapies to treat poor health successfully.

Naturopaths see childhood diseases, such as mumps and chickenpox, as a necessary evil in building up a strong immune system. Diet, rather than vaccination, is considered an important way of boosting the body's defences and, during times of illness, the child is nursed with natural remedies.

Naturopathy can help with conditions such as allergies, bronchitis, eczema and other skin diseases. It can also improve your child's resistance to infection.

the first treatment

The initial consultation generally takes about an hour. The naturopath will address the key health concerns facing your child, so that any underlying imbalances can be pinpointed. She will ask questions about your child's lifestyle and medical history, as well as any particular recent problems that have been troubling him. She may then use several different diagnostic techniques according to what she specializes in. She may also carry out routine medical checks, such as blood and urine tests.

The naturopath will then recommend a course of treatment based on what she has discovered about your child. This usually takes the form of nutritional guidance because diet is the most important element in naturopathy. To help specific health problems, she may prescribe a special diet, for example one that eliminates trigger foods, such as wheat or dairy products. Ideally, foods should be vegetarian, organic and raw wherever possible. The rest of the treatment may consist of a combination of different therapies, such as osteopathy and homeopathy, depending on the nature of your child's complaint. The length of treatment will depend on the illness.

how does naturopathy work?

A multidisciplinary approach that blends Eastern and Western natural therapies, naturopathy encourages healing to take place on all levels and creates a powerful new way of working with your body. The aim is to boost health by making the immune system stronger and more resistant to disease.

Naturopaths believe in treating the whole person by using a combination of techniques, including nutritional medicine, Western herbalism, acupuncture, homeopathy, iridology, kinesiology, reflexology, massage, aromatherapy and flower remedies. They devote time and care to each patient, whom they regard as a holistic unity of body, mind and spirit. In using a range of alternative methods of diagnosis, naturopaths can often successfully pinpoint a predisposition to disease before its onset, and they are therefore able to treat it with specific therapies and changes to the patient's lifestyle.

A naturopath often sees herself in the role of a teacher, whose job it is to educate and support the patient. The treatment varies according to the individual patient and the naturopath's areas of expertise. These may include reflexology, acupressure, acupuncture, hydrotherapy (the use of water, both internally and externally, to boost health and well-being and treat certain ailments), nutrition, herbal remedies and homeopathic remedies.

western herbalism

Herbalism – the use of plant remedies in the treatment of disease – is the oldest known form of medicine. Current developments in science are revealing interesting information about the active ingredients of these plants; for example, echinacea has now been shown to prevent colds in 32 separate studies.

Herbalism is now one of the most widely used complementary therapies. Over 80 per cent of the world's population rely on herbs for health in some way, and an increasing number of people in the Western world are turning to it as a kinder alternative to mainstream medicine. You can use herbal medicine in two ways: to speed up your body's healing process; then continue with herbal therapy to protect yourself in the long-term.

Modern Western herbalism centres on the belief that plants have a vital energy that benefits the body by boosting its self-healing abilities. Plants have the ability to rebalance the body, giving us a surge of energy that can help prevent illness.

Herbalism is a holistic therapy, meaning that it looks at the whole person not just the symptoms of disease. As with homeopathy, two children could visit the same herbalist, with apparently the same condition, but leave with totally different prescriptions. Herbalists treat people as individuals, believing that this approach gets the best results.

Preparation of herbal remedies

Dried and fresh herbs, herbal teas and other herbal preparations are widely available in health-food stores and supermarkets. There are three ways to prepare them.

Herbal teas (also known as 'tisanes') Pour 250 ml (9 fl. oz) boiling water over 1 teaspoonful of dried flowers, stems or leaves, or 2 teaspoonsful of fresh material. Stir and leave for a couple of minutes or longer, according to taste. Strain and drink when cool. The recommended dosage for children is 50 ml (2 fl. oz). Infusions can also be added to bath water, using 10–20 times this dosage.

Decoctions Place 1 tablespoonful of powdered root, seeds or bark in 600 ml (20 fl. oz) of water, simmering for 30 minutes, then strain before drinking. The recommended dosage for children is 50 ml (2 fl. oz). Like infusions, these can be added to bath water, using 10–20 times this dosage.

Tinctures Place 200 g (7 oz) dried flowers in an airtight jar and pour over 1 litre (35 fl. oz) of a water and alcohol mixture. Leave for at least two weeks, shaking daily. Strain into a dark bottle. Add ½ teaspoon to water, juice or herbal tea.

uses of western herbalism

Children suffering from a wide range of conditions can benefit from Western herbalism, which is often used in conjunction with conventional medicine. It can be used to treat almost any childhood ailment, ranging from skin problems, such as psoriasis and eczema, to allergic responses, such as hay fever, allergic rhinitis and asthma.

the first treatment

The first consultation generally takes about an hour. The herbalist will take notes on your child's medical history and begin to build up a picture of her as an individual. Healing is a matter of teamwork, with patient, practitioner and the prescribed treatment all working together to restore the body to health. The herbalist may also give advice about diet and lifestyle. Herbalists prescribe from a wide range of plant-based materials, which are used both internally and externally, and which include preparations such as tinctures, syrups, capsules and creams. The second appointment is usually 2 weeks later, followed by monthly appointments, depending on the individual case.

how does western herbalism work?

Medical herbalists are trained in the same diagnostic skills as doctors, but they take a more holistic approach. When addressing a problem, they seek to identify the underlying cause, and it is the cause that they treat rather than the symptoms alone. The thinking behind this is that suppression of symptoms is not sufficient to rid the body of the disease. Herbalists use their remedies to restore the balance of the body, thus enabling it to mobilize its own healing powers.

Herbal remedies are extracts of part of the plant, such as the leaves, roots or berries, and they contain hundreds, perhaps thousands, of plant substances. Herbalists believe that there is a balance between the active ingredients in the plant and that their action is enhanced by the many other substances present (known as the synergistic effect). Remedies are therefore prepared in a way that utilizes all the substances in the plant. This is in contrast to conventional drugs, which tend to be prepared by isolating the active ingredient.

Extracts of plants with an affinity for a particular part of the body are used to 'feed' the body. As the body is strengthened, so is its ability to fight disease, and when balance is restored, good health will follow.

Warning Herbs can be powerful and may have serious side-effects. Always consult a qualified medical herbalist and your doctor before using them. If your child shows any unusual reactions after taking a herbal remedy, stop giving it to her immediately and consult your herbalist or doctor.

bach flower remedies

These safe, gentle remedies, developed by Dr Edward Bach in the 1930s, now have a huge following around the world. They are holistic in approach and work by treating the patient not the disease. They are often used in conjunction with other therapies, particularly homeopathy.

uses of flower remedies

As long as you follow the instructions, babies and children can be given flower remedies with complete safety and good results. Practitioners regard Bach flower remedies as suitable for children with a variety of physical and emotional conditions. They provide good supportive therapy for the emotional aspects of illness, such as anxiety, which are so important to the recovery process. The remedies also play a preventive role in times of stress and anxiety and can help when children are generally 'under the weather' but no specific problem has been diagnosed.

Dr Bach was very keen on the notion of self-help. The remedies are suitable for using at home because, in most cases, diagnosis and treatment is easy. However, if you have any doubts, consult a practitioner before embarking on a course of treatment for your child.

Bach flower remedies

The various remedies (such as Aspen, Mimulus, Gentian, Mustard) are divided into seven groups, which represent the main spheres of conflict affecting health. These are:

Group 1 Fear

Group 2 Uncertainty

Group 3 Lack of interest in present circumstances

Group 4 Loneliness

Group 5 Over-sensitivity to influences and ideas

Group 6 Despondency or despair

Group 7 Over-concern for the welfare of others.

the first treatment

The practitioner will choose remedies for a child in exactly the same way as she does for an adult. During the initial consultation, she will write a full report, detailing various aspects of your child's physical and emotional health and well-being. She will ask the child to describe how he feels. His personality and current situation will guide the practitioner to the appropriate remedy, and she will observe your child closely to try to assess his state of mind. She will then select a remedy that she thinks best matches your child's mood.

how do flower remedies work?

Like other forms of natural medicine, flower remedies work by treating the individual, not the disease itself, nor the symptoms of the disease. They work specifically on the emotional condition of the patient. The effect of the remedies is to turn negative attitudes into positive ones, thus freeing up your child's system to fully fight disease.

Dr Bach believed that state of mind plays a vital role in maintaining health and recovering from illness, a claim backed many times over by scientists. He devised a system of 37 flower remedies, prepared from the flowers of wild plants, trees and bushes, plus one remedy (Rock Water), which is pure water. There is also a combination called Rescue Remedy, which is designed specifically for helping people to cope with difficult and demanding situations, and which is often referred to as the 39th remedy. However, anyone can use the remedies, at any time, to restore the balance of their body.

The remedies are prepared by steeping freshly picked flowers in pure spring water and leaving them in full sunlight for a couple of hours, during which time the water is imbued with the energy of the plant. This solution is then diluted and mixed with a small amount of alcohol.

The remedies may be taken on their own or in conjunction with other treatments, both medical and otherwise, as they will not clash. They are safe, non-addictive, have no side-effects and can be taken by children of all ages – even newborns. However, they are not a substitute for medical treatment, so if symptoms persist, consult your doctor.

When choosing a Bach remedy, forget about your child's symptoms. Instead, focus solely on his emotions and how he feels. For example, there is no remedy for a headache, as such. Instead, concentrate on how the headache is making him feel.

There are many childhood illnesses for which particular remedies are highly effective, and it is important to consider each child's needs individually. For example, a shy child, who may suffer from anxiety and related symptoms, probably has a Mimulus personality. This means he will fear everyday things such as the dark, dogs and so on, and be nervous, timid and generally shy.

Dosage

Remedies are preserved in alcohol. For this reason, you should dilute them before giving them to your child. The dosage is generally 2 drops added to a glass of water (double the amount for Rescue Remedy). You can also add the remedy to milk or fruit juice. Give four times a day until you see an improvement in the condition.

eastern therapies

traditional chinese medicine

Traditional Chinese medicine (TCM) is one of the great medical systems of the world, with a history going back to the 3rd century BC. TCM is an umbrella term covering Chinese herbalism (see page 33), acupuncture and acupressure (see pages 34–35), dietary therapy and exercises in breathing and movement (tai chi and chi gong). One or several of these may be employed in the course of treatment.

In recent years, its popularity in the West has grown rapidly. It still forms a major part of health-care provision in China, where it is offered in state hospitals alongside Western medicine.

uses of traditional chinese medicine

TCM benefits people of any age and can be used for a wide range of conditions. Among the more commonly treated disorders are skin diseases, such as eczema and urticaria, and respiratory conditions, including asthma, bronchitis and coughs.

the first treatment

Before deciding on a particular treatment and its course, practitioners take into account any previous or current illness and medication. In the case of children, they will adjust the level of treatment accordingly.

how does traditional chinese medicine work?

TCM is based on the concepts of yin and yang. It aims to understand and treat the many ways in which the fundamental balance and harmony between the two may be undermined, and the ways in which a person's life force, or *chi*, may be depleted or blocked. Treatment is based on the diagnosis of patterns of signs and symptoms that reflect an imbalance.

It also places great emphasis on lifestyle management as a preventive measure, recognizing that health is more than just the absence of disease. TMC can be used to enhance well-being and happiness.

Research studies

Studies show that many herbs have potential as drugs. A trial conducted in Germany in 2004, showed that Chinese herbal medicine combined with acupuncture reduced hay-fever symptoms.

Warning TMC is unregulated in some countries. Make sure you choose a registered practitioner through a recognized body.

chinese herbalism

Chinese herbalism is an ancient form of healing that is often used in conjunction with acupuncture and acupressure (see pages 34–35). Part of traditional Chinese medicine, the philosophy is the same: the treatment works by restoring harmony and health to mind and body. If your child has ever had liver problems, such as jaundice, be sure to tell the practitioner because some herbs can have an adverse effect.

uses of chinese herbalism

Children of all ages can benefit and a wide number of complaints respond well to treatment, including eczema, urticaria and respiratory conditions such as asthma and bronchitis. When treating children, the practitioner will make suitable adjustments to the dosages and take other relevant factors into account.

the first treatment

Choose a fully trained and registered practitioner who is qualified to treat children. He will begin by thoroughly examining your child, with an emphasis on observation. He will also ask you some quite detailed questions. He will then prescribe one herb or a combination of herbs, according to what he feels is the most appropriate remedy.

Herbs are now available in a number of forms, both traditional and modern. Traditionally they are provided as a tea, made by boiling a mixture of dried herbs in water, or as pills. Herbs are also prescribed as freeze-dried powders or tinctures. The herbs taste unusual at first – they are often bitter – but most people quickly get used to this. You can try sweetening teas and tinctures with honey to make them more palatable for children.

how does chinese herbalism work?

Chinese herbal medicine, along with the other components of TMC, is based on the concepts of yin and yang. It aims to understand and treat the many ways in which the fundamental balance and harmony between the two may be undermined, and the ways in which a person's life force, or chi, may be blocked. Treatment is based on the diagnosis of the signs and symptoms that reflect the imbalance.

Herbal medicine is different from pharmaceutical medicine. It is far less likely to cause side-effects and, because herbs are usually prescribed in combination, they undergo a synergy that increases their effectiveness. Herbal medicine seeks primarily to correct internal imbalances rather than treating the symptoms alone, and is designed to encourage your body's self-healing process.

acupuncture

Acupuncture, which is part of traditional Chinese medicine, is an holistic approach to the management of disease and the maintenance of health that dates back over two thousand years. It works on the energy of the body, by inserting fine needles into key points to disperse blockages and bring about an improvement in a specific complaint. Western-style acupuncture (also known as medical acupuncture) is a comparatively recent development that uses a more limited range of techniques based on Western medical diagnoses.

uses of acupuncture

Acupuncture can be of particular help to children with allergies, asthma and bronchitis. It also provides pain relief as it activates the body's 'feel-good' chemicals (known as endorphins). People also find that it leads to increased energy levels, improved sleep patterns, and an enhanced sense of well-being. Be sure to choose an acupuncturist who has experience of dealing with children.

the first treatment

Your child should wear loose, comfortable clothing because the acupuncturist may need to access points on the body, arms and legs. She will need to find out about your child's general state of health in order to identify the underlying pattern of disharmony. You will be asked about your child's current symptoms and treatment, his medical history, including that of the immediate family, and his diet, digestive system, sleep patterns and emotional state.

To discover how the energies are flowing in your child's body, the acupuncturist will probably feel the pulses on both wrists. The structure, colour and coating of the tongue also give an insight into your child's health.

Acupuncture needles are much finer than the needles used in conventional medicine. The sensation when a needle is inserted is a tingling or dull ache. The needles are left in place either for a second or two, or longer depending on the effect required. There are about 500 acupuncture points on the body, and an acupuncturist generally selects perhaps 10 or 12 of these for each treatment.

how does acupuncture work?

Acupuncture can be used to treat people with a wide range of illnesses. Its focus is on improving well-being, rather than the isolated treatment of specific symptoms. According to traditional Chinese philosophy, health is dependent on the body's motivating energy – known as *chi* – moving in a smooth and balanced way through a series of meridians (channels) beneath the skin. *Chi* consists of equal and opposite qualities – yin and yang – and any imbalance between these can result in illness.

The flow of *chi* can be disturbed by a number of factors. These include anxiety and stress, poor nutrition, hereditary factors, and infections. The principal aim of acupuncture is to treat the whole person by restoring the equilibrium between his physical, emotional and spiritual aspects.

acupressure

Part of traditional Chinese medicine, acupressure is particularly suitable for treating babies and young children. It is a hands-on method that involves the application of fingertip pressure rather than needles to the appropriate acupuncture points. Massage and tapping with a rounded probe are also techniques suitable for children and those with a fear of needles.

uses of acupressure

Acupressure is particularly effective for stress and anxiety-related illnesses, including insomnia, headaches and digestive upsets. It helps to release tension from the muscles and boosts the natural circulation.

the first treatment

The practitioner will take detailed notes about your child's life-style and diet. She will also take his pulse. Your child will remain fully clothed and will lie down on a couch. The practitioner will then proceed to apply pressure, using her thumbs, fingers, palms and sometimes even feet.

Your child may experience slight discomfort, but this will be momentary. Generally, people feel well after an acupressure session. This is because it stimulates the production of the 'feel-good' endorphins, which leads to a sense of well-being.

The practitioner will then arrive at a final diagnosis by piecing together all the information that she has gathered. A session usually lasts for about 30 minutes for a child, and you should expect to have weekly appointments at first.

how does acupressure work?

Acupressure works in a very similar way to acupuncture. It involves using pressure on the acupuncture points – sensitive areas at certain points on the surface of the body. The practitioner uses mostly light thumb and fingertip pressure.

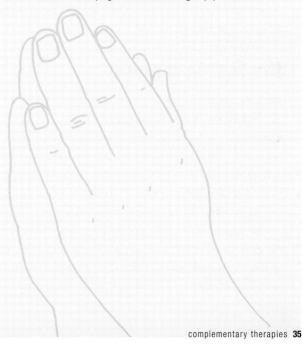

ayurvedic medicine

Ayurveda is an ancient system of medicine practised in India. Roughly translated, the word 'ayurveda' means 'life knowledge'. It is a traditional holistic system that places equal emphasis on treating mind, body and spirit. Treatment is based on balancing *prana*, the internal energy that promotes health and well-being. Food is of particular importance to children, and ayurvedic medicine believes that many childhood maladies stem from what is happening in the stomach.

uses of ayurvedic medicine

Ayurveda can be used successfully to treat many ailments. It is particularly beneficial for digestive complaints, such as constipation, and skin complaints, such as eczema. In addition, Indian head massage is a great aid to relaxation.

the first treatment

The practitioner will first want to build up a picture of your child and will ask questions about her lifestyle, diet and digestive system, likes and dislikes. He will observe your child's appearance, particularly her skin, hair and nails, studying her face and noting how she talks and her body language. He will also take your child's pulse to further help to determine her constitutional type.

how does ayurvedic medicine work?

Your individual constitution and how it relates to your energies is the key to good health. If your constitution is weak then you become ill. Each of us has a unique constitution, determined by the balance of three vital energies, or *doshas*: *vata*, *pitta* and *kapha*. Practitioners believe that disease is caused by an imbalance of these energies, and that each of us is governed by a particular energy. This energy therefore determines not only your child's constitution but also her temperament, hair colour and even her weight.

As it is a complete system of medicine, treatment usually consists of several different approaches. These may include: making changes to your child's diet, detoxification, herbal remedies to correct imbalances, massage, breathing exercises and yoga.

yoga

Yoga is a practical technique for developing both mind and body. Children benefit from learning how to develop mind and body awareness, and from thinking about their breathing. Yoga stimulates the body's energy centres and the endocrine system, which is especially important for children because it determines both how fast they grow and their emotional health. In addition, yoga poses increase the intake of oxygen into the bloodstream, improving health and wellbeing.

Children love yoga because so many of the poses imitate forms found in nature, such as trees and animals, which turns it into a fun activity for them.

uses of yoga

Everyone, both young and old, can benefit from yoga sessions with a qualified instructor. It can help stress-related problems, such as poor sleep patterns and asthma. Yoga is not a therapy as such, so teachers are not governed by a professional body.

the first treatment

Dress your child in comfortable, non-restrictive clothes that are warm enough as they may become distracted by feeling restricted or too cold when relaxing at the end of the session.

how does yoga work?

The aim is to create a harmonious balance of mind, body and spirit by means of a combination of breathing techniques, postures and meditation.

Prana, the vital energy force, is everywhere, and our bodies absorb it from the food we eat, from sunlight and from the air we breathe. This energy flows through energy centres, known as *chakras*, to all our major organs. Seven major *chakras* are located down the spinal column, from the crown of the head to the base of the spine, each with a particular emotional, spiritual or psychological link. How each *chakra* functions depends very much on a person's physical and mental health, and practising yoga can help to shift blockages and rebalance our *chakras*.

In India, children traditionally start to practise yoga at about 8 years old. However, yoga can also be taught to children as young as 3 years, although it is best to keep it fun by introducing an element of play. Bear this in mind when practising yoga with your own children: with those aged 3–6 years, concentrate on the fun element and work on developing their muscles, and with children aged 7–11 years, attempt more difficult poses.

How yoga can benefit your child

• The breathing that she uses in yoga makes full use of her lungs, boosting energy and improving circulation. It also teaches her how to breathe correctly.

• The poses tone, strengthen and exercise her muscles, releasing pent-up tension and encouraging flexibility.

• Yoga improves her posture, body awareness and sleep patterns.

active therapies

the alexander technique

The Alexander technique is concerned with the way we move, our posture and how we coordinate our actions in everyday life. It works on the belief that we are held upright by a dynamic tension that works in tandem with gravity. Correct poise is therefore a question of finding the right balance of tensions. By correctly controlling the position of our head, neck and back, it is possible to achieve good posture. Young children have a lot of natural poise and balance, and move gracefully, but they can still benefit from using the Alexander technique as a preventive method. Many develop poor posture when they start school and begin to sit hunched over a desk or computer screen. Slouching in front of the television and lack of exercise do not help either.

uses of the alexander technique

By improving posture and movement, the Alexander technique can help with 'mechanical' problems, such as back and neck pain. It can also help with stress-related conditions, such as headaches, breathing problems and stomach problems.

The technique is widely used by physiotherapists, midwives and other health professionals, as well as by actors, singers, dancers and athletes to improve their performance.

Children generally respond well to the style of instruction, and you might consider taking lessons yourself, so that you can work through the exercises with your child.

the first treatment

Lessons are on a one-to-one basis. The teacher will observe your child and work with him to achieve improved posture and lightness of movement. She will run through some basic techniques with your child, asking him to carry out various movements, such as sitting, bending and walking. She will point out any bad habits and show your child the correct way to move, for example when getting up from a chair.

Your child will learn new ways of using his body that keep his spine free of tension. At the end of the lesson he may well feel that he is walking taller and is more relaxed. After several lessons, he will be able to work on his posture without the guidance of a teacher.

how does the alexander technique work?

The technique aims to change established patterns of poor posture and movement by subtly lengthening the spine. Teachers guide students through various movements, using verbal instructions and light touch to improve their coordination and balance. This reduces tension and fatigue, relieves pain, improves various medical conditions and generally promotes well-being. Students are then encouraged to use what they learn in everyday life.

For our bodies to function correctly, there must be a proper relationship between our head, neck and spine, known as 'primary control'. When under stress, the body goes into 'survival mode' and tension rapidly builds in the neck muscles, causing a knock-on hunched effect, and spreads throughout the rest of the body. When the neck is free of tension, the head is poised on top of the neck and the spine is lengthened. Once this relationship is established, everything else tends to fall into place.

Often referred to as 'posture training', the Alexander technique is not a therapy but instead is taught in a teacher–pupil scenario. The approach is a holistic one, the idea being that the mind and body form a whole, and addresses the source of the problem not the symptoms.

relaxation & visualization

Both doctors and complementary practitioners encourage relaxation as a means of dealing with stress and overcoming stress-related illness. While there are many different ways of relaxing, the end result is the same: total relaxation of mind and body for a set period of time. The idea is that if your mind is relaxed, your body will follow suit. This is a therapy that children respond particularly well to.

uses of relaxation

Relaxation can help with sleep problems, headaches, nausea and vomiting, stress and anxiety, asthma and other breathing-related difficulties, and constipation. Relaxation and visualization techniques are safe for everyone, even very young children.

the first treatment

The practitioner will start by taking your child's medical history and asking for details about her lifestyle that may indicate the cause of her anxiety. He will then ask your child to sit on a chair or lie on a couch, shut her eyes and concentrate on her breathing, taking deep breaths until she feels calm. The room should be quiet with no background noises to disturb the session, which will probably begin with a basic 'tense-and-release' exercise.

To do this, he will talk your child through focusing on each major muscle group, usually starting with the arms or legs, tensing the muscles for about 10 seconds and then releasing and relaxing them one by one. He will instruct your child to work around her body, repeating this action.

Some practitioners may ask your child to imagine a special place, such as an enchanted wood, the idea being that the child can retreat to this special place whenever she is troubled.

The success of the session largely depends on your child's willingness to cooperate. The session will end with a period of rest to enable your child's body to return to normal. Once you have mastered the basics, you can carry out relaxation sessions at home with your child as and when the need arises.

how does relaxation work?

When the body enters a state of relaxation, mental and physical tension is released, boosting feelings of well-being. Children respond particularly to this because it encourages them to use their imagination.

When the body is relaxed, the heart rate slows, breathing becomes more regular and adrenaline levels are reduced. This allows the immune system to function more efficiently, thereby helping the body to fight disease more effectively. Relaxation frees the mind from stress, which allows the muscles to relax.

True relaxation is a therapeutic healing process that focuses on calming both mind and body. Feelings of calm replace those of tension, fear and anxiety. Once your child has learned the simple techniques of relaxation, she can practise them anywhere and it doesn't necessarily have to be lying down with her eyes closed.

Relaxation techniques

Relaxation works by rebalancing the nervous system. There are several basic techniques, some of which are suitable for children:

Tense-and-release exercises Working around the body, first tense then release each muscle group in turn. This is the basis of many relaxation techniques (see above).

Passive muscular relaxation Focus your attention on a particular muscle group, feel the tension, then release it. This can be practised anywhere – you do not have to be lying down.

Visualization This mental relaxation technique involves imagining a special place to which you can escape when troubled (see above). Forming positive peaceful associations promotes healing and well-being, and overcomes negative feelings.

Deeper relaxation techniques These include hypnotherapy, meditation, autogenics and biofeedback, all of which result in a trance-like state.

arts therapies

Arts therapies can help children who are in need of emotional support, for example during times of stress. Children generally respond well to this type of stimulation, which helps them to convey ideas and emotions that they may find difficult to put into words. There are four main therapies: dance, art, drama and music, all of which have proved useful therapeutic tools in helping children to express themselves.

uses of arts therapies

Children who are experiencing social, emotional or physical problems can benefit from finding an outlet for self-expression. Arts therapies can be of particular help to those suffering from anxiety and stress. Studies show that music therapy is particularly beneficial for hyperactive children.

This non-verbal way of revealing deeper emotions that may not otherwise be clearly expressed can be a useful device to encourage children to open up. It is also useful as a tool for personal growth and greater self-understanding.

the first treatment

A session is usually on a one-to-one basis and lasts about 30 minutes. The therapist will start by assessing your child and finding out what you hope to achieve. Sessions usually comprise a period of creative activity, plus time for reflection and discussion. However, there is no set structure, and the course of the therapy will be determined by your child's needs and the approach that the therapist decides to take.

The therapist will encourage your child to express himself freely through art, and the resulting images can help to reveal any suppressed emotions or conflicts. Reflecting on these images can help her to understand and deal with the issues that arise.

Therapy may last for a few months or many years, depending on the particular situation. The emphasis during treatment is on the self-expression of the individual rather than any teacher/pupil relationship.

how do arts therapies work?

Arts therapies work by helping children to explore their feelings in order to deal with psychological problems that may be holding them back in life. The choice of therapy is usually dictated by children's personal preference. The therapist will then encourage them to express themselves through the arts. She will create an environment in which children feel comfortable about exploring their thoughts.

There are two main approaches:

• The first regards the act of creating the artwork as therapeutic in itself, allowing your child to understand his own inner conflicts and emotions without any interpretation from the therapist.

• The second takes the view that the artwork is a non-verbal method of communication that enables the therapist to interpret and identify your child's needs so that she can help him deal with the issues.

Arts therapies and their benefits

There are a number of different therapies, all aimed at promoting self-expression.

Art helps children to communicate through the creative use of paint, clay and other materials.

Dance encourages children to express themselves through bodily movement.

Music provides children with the opportunity to express themselves through singing and/or playing musical instruments.

Drama enables children to act out their thoughts and feelings, building their confidence and awareness.

manipulative therapies

chiropractic

Chiropractic basically addresses the skeletal system and the effects that misalignment has on the nervous system and the body as a whole. By correcting the alignment of the spine and joints, chiropractors reduce the strain on the muscles and release trapped nerves, encouraging the body's self-healing processes. Chiropractic does not involve the use of any drugs or surgery.

uses of chiropractic

Children benefit greatly from chiropractic, and it is suitable for treating a range of mechanical problems affecting the joints and muscles. Indeed, those with lower-back pain have been shown to derive more benefit from chiropractic than hospital treatment. Conditions suitable for chiropractic include: neck pain, tension headaches, back pain, joint problems, sprains and ankle injuries.

Warning Chiropractic is not suitable for children who have recently suffered any fractures.

the first treatment

In order to reach a diagnosis, the chiropractor will first build up a case history of your child. This involves all or some of the following: a through physical examination of your child, observation of her posture, examination of her joints, standard tests and, if necessary, X-rays. You will be encouraged to bring a letter of referral from your child's doctor, together with details of any previous investigations, treatment or X-rays.

When treating your child, the chiropractor will use a range of manipulative techniques designed to improve the function of the joints, thus relieving pain and muscle spasm. These usually involve putting pressure on a particular area. He will direct the manipulation at specific joints in order to reduce muscle strains and improve mobility.

The chiropractor will support this treatment by offering counselling and advice about your child's lifestyle, diet, exercise and posture, in order to help in managing the condition and to prevent a recurrence of the problem.

how does chiropractic work?

Chiropractors treat problems of the joints, bones and muscles, and their effects on the nervous system. Working on all the joints of the body, concentrating particularly on the spine, they use their hands to make gentle 'adjustments' (the chiropractic term for manipulation) to improve the efficiency of the nervous system and release the body's natural healing ability.

In comparison with osteopaths and physiotherapists, chiropractors tend to use manipulation as the main form of treatment, relying less on soft tissue and massage techniques.

osteopathy

Osteopathy is a holistic therapy that works on the body's skeletal, muscular and nervous systems, manipulating misaligned bones and joints in order to relieve pain, improve mobility and restore the natural balance of the body. The psychological benefits of touch and the physical benefits of manipulation combine to give very effective results.

uses of osteopathy

Osteopathy can benefit children of all ages and with a wide range of conditions, such as glue ear and insomnia, as well as being particularly effective for colic and spinal joint pain. It can, for example, reduce the need for medication, lessen the psychological effects of an operation or serious illness and assist recovery, as well as helping premature babies. This treatment is popular with parents because it does not involve any drugs or invasive techniques that can cause side-effects or possible problems in later life.

the first treatment

Osteopathy clinics are designed to make children feel safe and relaxed, and treatment is often communal because it is more reassuring. The osteopath will assess how well your child's body is functioning before taking details of her medical history. He will ask you about her complaint or symptoms and general development.

The osteopath will then examine your child, which usually involves some simple movements and exercises to assess her joints, muscles and tissue. He will place his hands on your child to see how she moves, assessing different parts of the body and different movements. The first appointment usually lasts about

50 minutes and further sessions last between 20 and 50 minutes. Most new patients will need further treatment. This is not something you can try at home and must always be carried out by a registered practitioner.

how does osteopathy work?

Osteopathy is a way of detecting and treating damaged parts of the body, such as muscles, ligaments, nerves and joints. The body works most efficiently, with minimum wear and tear, when it is in balance. Paediatric osteopathy is a very gentle manual technique that works to ensure that the framework of the child's body is in alignment, thus allowing a good blood and nerve supply to the internal organs, and relieving any tension in the muscles and bones that might restrict this.

It involves a variety of movements, including stretching and twisting actions. 'Cranial osteopathy' is the application of osteopathic treatment to the head. However, in the case of newborns and babies, the whole body must be treated for osteopathy to be effective – which is what paediatric osteopaths do. The therapy is based on the principle that all illnesses – minor or serious – are a result of an imbalance somewhere in the network of systems in the body.

massage therapy

Massage harnesses the therapeutic use of touch to bring comfort, warmth and reassurance, all of which can have a profoundly positive effect on the physical and emotional well-being of your child. Therapists take a holistic view, using a variety of movements and techniques to form a bond between themselves and their patient.

Massage is a comforting and soothing therapy, and one that children find particularly enjoyable. It is a form of touch that enables the body to relax, thus triggering a sense of well-being. More vigorous forms of massage can free up tense muscles and help with stiff joints.

uses of massage therapy

All children, including young babies, benefit from massage, and they do not necessarily have to be ill. It helps with fatigue, stress, back pain, shoulders and neck, muscle stiffness, and tension and anxiety. Babies are particularly responsive to massage, and it can be used to soothe them during times of illness. It also reinforces the bonding process between parent and child.

Massage has two key benefits: it soothes common childhood complaints and comforts a fractious child. Massage with essential oils, such as eucalyptus and lavender, will help to clear the sinuses and combat coughs, colds and congestion. It soothes wind, colic and constipation, and can help teething children to settle. In addition, if your child has difficulty in sleeping, he will find a loving touch very reassuring.

the first treatment

The therapist will ask you about your child's health and any problems, past or present, that might be affecting him. She will also ask you about your child's lifestyle – his dietary habits, sleep patterns, exercise regime and stress levels. When you are looking for a practitioner, it is always advisable to see their relevant qualifications first and, if you are in any doubt, to discuss your child's treatment.

To familiarize your child with the sensation of massage, the therapist will start with soft, gentle strokes all over his body. To achieve a free-flowing motion, she will generally use a carrier oil, such as grape-seed or sweet almond oil. She will then move to his back, using gentle stoking movements with the flat of her hand. This movement not only warms up the skin but also makes sure that the oil is spread evenly. She will then move on to rubbing and kneading the muscles and connective tissue to loosen any knots, sometimes using a hand-over-hand technique. Next, she may use deep pressure strokes, depending on your child's age and the nature of the problem.

Once you have visited a therapist and received her diagnosis and recommendations, you can continue to massage your child at home. This is a great way of bonding with your child, and he will find it very comforting if he is sick. However, an unwell child may simply prefer just to be held and have his hair stroked lightly, or his hands and feet gently kneaded – techniques that are both relaxing and comforting.

Warning Tell your therapist if your child has a nut allergy before the start a massage session. Almond oil, which is often used in massage, could cause potentially serious problems for children who are sensitive to nuts.

how does massage therapy work?

The skin is the largest sensory organ of the body, and the messages that it receives are sent to the brain via the nervous system. Massaging the skin therefore has an effect on the whole body, including the heart and the circulatory and respiratory systems. It can also help to eliminate toxins from the body and improve muscle tone.

Massage releases the 'feel-good' chemicals (endorphins) that are the body's natural painkillers, and studies in Norway have shown that the levels of these chemicals increase after a massage. As stress levels go down, the body's natural healing abilities kick in.

Massage stimulates the circulation of blood and lymph, and reduces blood pressure, heart rate and muscle tension, resulting in a deep feeling of relaxation and well-being. More blood flows to the muscles as they relax and then, when they contract, this blood is pumped back to the heart, thus boosting the circulation. Massage also reduces the amount of the stress hormone (cortisol) in the bloodstream, opens the pores, promotes the elimination of toxins, and encourages muscular relaxation and joint flexibility, thus aiding mobility.

reflexology

Reflexology in its present form was developed in the twentieth century, although a similar therapy was used in China thousands of years ago. It is a safe, natural therapy based on the application of pressure to reflex points, mainly in the feet but also in the hands, the aim being to release any blockages of energy that are causing illness, thereby restoring the body's equilibrium and enabling it to heal itself. The effectiveness of this safe, natural therapy is recognized by doctors and health-care professionals everywhere.

uses of reflexology

Reflexology is suitable for children of all ages and can relieve a variety of conditions. It is particularly helpful in treating colic (see page 100) and constipation (see page 102). Since reflexology treats the whole person, not just the symptoms of disease, everyone can benefit from treatment. A preventive therapy, it can also help with acute and chronic illness, stress-related conditions, sleep disorders, back pain and digestive disorders.

An increasing number of people are using reflexology as a means of relaxing, balancing and harmonizing the body as well. Indeed, after a course of reflexology for a specific condition, many people decide to continue with regular treatments in order to maintain their health and well-being.

Research studies

A study conducted in Scotland in 2001 showed that reflexology was very successful in treating children with constipation, triggering further, on-going research. Studies repeatedly show that the power of hands-on touch is especially beneficial to children.

the first treatment

After discussing your child's problem with you, the reflexologist will begin to work on your child's feet, or hands if necessary, noting any problem areas.

Using his hands, he will apply pressure to her feet. Your child may feel some localized discomfort, but this will be momentary and it is an indication of congestion or imbalance in the corresponding part of the body. For the most part, she will find the sensation pleasant and soothing.

A treatment session usually lasts from 30 to 60 minutes. The course of treatment will vary in length, according to your child's needs, and the reflexologist will discuss this with you at the first session. After a couple of treatments, your child may respond very positively with a feeling of well-being and relaxation. Occasionally she may feel lethargic, nauseous or tearful, but this will soon pass. Either response provides vital information for the reflexologist because it shows how your child's body is responding to treatment.

how does reflexology work?

Reflexologists divide the body into ten channels, or zones, five on each side of the body, which run from the head to the feet. Energy flows freely through these channels when the individual is healthy but any blockages result in illness. The reflex points on the feet correspond to specific parts of the body, so the feet act as a map of the body.

Massage and pressure on the feet stimulate the whole body, including the nervous and circulatory systems. While he is applying pressure to the feet, the reflexologist can detect any tiny deposits or imbalances and, by working on these points, will release blockages and restore the free flow of energy through the whole body. This eases tension and improves circulation, thus encouraging the body to heal itself. The type of treatment, and its effects, will be different for every child.

Introducing your child to reflexology

It is easy to introduce a young child to reflexology. Although it is best to start when she is a baby, any time before the age of 2 years is good. Once she is a little older, she may be less co-operative! However, it is important to persevere as reflexology will comfort and reassure your child, calming her and helping her to relax in a variety of situations.

common ailments

introduction

The ailments covered in this book are common childhood complaints, although most affect adults too. What they all have in common is their suitability for complementary treatment.

The ailments are divided into five categories according to the part of the body that they affect. Each ailment generally includes a list of common symptoms, a list of triggers or causes, an outline of the treatments offered by conventional medicine, descriptions of suitable complementary treatments, plus some common-sense suggestions.

Most complementary treatments can be used in conjunction with conventional treatment as part of an integrated approach and offer a valuable means of support for the health and well-being of your child.

contents

first aid box

cuts & grazes

Minor cuts and grazes, where the skin is broken and there is some tissue damage and bleeding, which can be treated at home.

treatment

• Wash the wound carefully under cold running water to remove any traces of dirt or grit, and gently pat dry. Alternatively, add a few drops of antiseptic tea tree essential oil to a bowl of water and use this to bathe the wound. Do not put undiluted essential oil on the cut because this will sting.

• If there is any swelling, wrap a few ice cubes in a face cloth and hold it against the affected area.

• Gently press the wound with a clean cloth or gauze pad to stop any bleeding. Dab on a little calendula cream, which has antiseptic properties.

• Apply a dressing or plaster.

• The homeopathic remedy Arnica can be used for shock and bruising.

Warning If the bleeding does not stop after 10 minutes, or the wound is gaping and requires stitches, take your child straight to hospital.

insect stings & bites

These are painful but seldom serious. However, swelling from a sting inside the mouth may result in breathing difficulties and, on rare occasions, the child may develop an allergic reaction: both require emergency medical treatment.

treatment

• If you can see a sting, quickly pull it out with tweezers.

• Cool the affected area under running water or hold a cold compress against it to reduce any pain or stinging. Neat lavender oil is soothing for insect bites. A mixture of 1 teaspoonful of cider vinegar and 2 drops of lavender essential oil helps to calm the inflammation from wasp or bee stings.

• The homeopathic remedy Arnica can be given to calm down your child. Apis is helpful with swelling and stinging.

Warning If the swelling gets worse or your child's breathing is affected, call an ambulance immediately.

sunburn

Over-exposure to sunlight causes burning of the skin, which may become red and sore, or even blistered, causing your child distress.

treatment

• Cover up your child immediately an move him into the shade.

• Give him a cooling drink to sip.

• Add 3–4 drops of lavender essential oil to cool water and use this to bathe any reddened skin.

• Make a soothing blend of 120 ml (4 fl. oz) of calamine lotion, 5 drops of German chamomile and 15 drops of lavender essential oil and apply to the affected area.

• The homeopathic remedy Sol helps with ill-effects from the sun, including mild sunburn. Belladonna is useful if there is high fever, hot burning skin and a headache. Apis can be used if the skin is swollen and puffy.

Warning If the skin has blistered, contact your doctor for advice.

burns

Burns are damage to the skin and underlying tissues. According to the amount of tissue damage, they vary in severity from minor (first-degree) burns where there is reddening and soreness of the skin but no blistering to extensive (third-degree) burns. Only minor burns are discussed here.

treatment

• Bathe or immerse the affected area in cold water until the burning sensation subsides. Keep the child as still as possible. Cover the burn with a sterile dressing to keep it clean. If in doubt contact your doctor for advice

• Lavender essential oil will cool burns. If there is no broken skin or blistering, dab a couple of drops of lavender oil directly on to the burn. If the skin is broken or blistered, dab lavender oil around the burn or make a compress to soothe the area. Put some lavender oil on a dry, cold cloth and cover the burn.

• The homeopathic remedy Arnica is helpful for any type of shock or trauma. Urtica urens is the remedy for minor burns. Calendula cream is soothing and also helps the skin to heal.

• Aloe vera gel will cool and soothe burns.

Warning If your child has a burn larger than 25 mm (1 in) in diameter, you should seek medical help immediately.

heatstroke

This occurs when a child gets over-heated in very hot weather, either from too much sun or from too much running around. The skin will be red-hot, and your child will experience headache, dizziness, nausea, and aches and pains. He may aslo feel drowsy and his pulse may quicken. In extreme cases the child can even become unconscious.

treatment

• If you think your child is suffering from sunstroke, take him into the shade and give him cool drinks to reduce his temperature.

• Keep babies out of the sun at all times.

• Make sure your child wears a sun hat.

• Children with fair complexions are at greater risk.

• Make sure your child drinks plenty of fluids because dehydration can lead to sunstroke. Give them plenty of cool drinks.

• Cool your child down by sponging his face and hands with tepid water.

• Use a fan to cool your child's face.

• Add a few drops each of lavender and eucalyptus essential oils to some cool water and use this to sponge down your child, avoiding his face.

The homeopathic remedy Sol is helpful for all ill-effects of the sun. It can also be given to children to build up their resistance to the sun. Belladonna is the correct remedy if there is a fever and throbbing headache

Warning This condition can be serious. If your child's temperature reaches 40°C (104°F), seek medical help immediately.

ringworm

Ringworm is caused by a highly infectious fungus (*Tinea*) that has nothing to do with worms. Nevertheless, it can be embarrassing for children because it is unsightly. It can spread rapidly around schools and nurseries, and is most common in children aged between 2 and 10 years.

Although not serious, the condition is very contagious so you should make sure your child does not come into contact with other children. Left untreated, ringworm can last for 6 weeks or even longer.

common symptoms

- Round or oval patches of skin, pale in the centre but redder and slightly raised towards the outside, where the fungus is active

- Affected area is sometimes dry and scaly, and can be itchy, sometimes becoming inflamed if scratched

- Most common on the face, although can also appear elsewhere, particularly on the groin, arms, legs and scalp

- Bald patches on the scalp, where the infection has caused the hair to break off

- Infection of the fingernails, caused by scratching

triggers & irritants

- Contact with the fungus, either by direct contact with infected skin, or indirectly, by sharing items, such as facecloths, with an infected individual

- Contact with pets – dogs and cats can carry the spores in their fur

- Exposure to warm, moist conditions, such as bathrooms and swimming pools, which are ideal for spreading the infection

conventional treatment

Take your child to the doctor if you are unsure about the cause of the rash, especially if it has not cleared up after a week. If ringworm is diagnosed, she will usually prescribe an anti-fungal cream, to be applied twice a day, usually for about 2 weeks.

complementary treatments

aromatherapy

One of the best ways of relieving itchy irritated skin is to apply a soothing aromatherapy mixture. And children will love the pure scent of essential oils.

• Neem is anti-fungal, and its leaves have antibacterial and anti-inflammatory properties. Try washing the affected area with neem soap.

• Tea tree oil also has anti-fungal qualities. Try diluting a couple of drops in a little carrier oil and applying three times a day to bring relief.

• For the skin, mix together 5 drops of tea tree, 5 drops of manuka and 8 drops of neem essential oils in 1 teaspoonful of sesame oil and gently rub into the affected area at night. You can also use this during the day if the ringworm is very itchy and bothering your child.

• For the scalp, mix together 5 drops of manuka, 10 drops of neem, 10 drops of tea tree, 5 drops of palmarosa and 5 drops of geranium essential oils. Add 4 drops of the mixture to 1 tablespoonful of sesame oil and apply to the scalp, making sure none comes into contact with the eyes, ears, nose and mouth. Leave for 10 minutes then shampoo.

homeopathy

It is always best to consult a qualified homeopath, who will take full account of your child's case history before making a diagnosis and recommending a treatment. Sepia is one of the most common remedies for ringworm, and tellurium is also used. Sulphur is useful for scalp infections.

naturopathy

• Add a little turmeric to aloe vera gel and apply to the skin.

• To help heal the skin, infuse 5 g (1 teaspoonful) of dried marigold flowers in 1 litre (1¼ pt) of boiling water for 5 minutes. Soak a cloth in the solution and apply to the affected area three times a day.

common sense

• Keep your child's towels and facecloths separate from the rest of the family.

• Dry your child's skin thoroughly after every bath.

• Choose loose-fitting, cotton clothing to avoid aggravating the condition.

• Apply a solution of vinegar, diluted in equal parts of water, to affected areas to help the skin to heal.

• Always wash your hands thoroughly after touching any infected areas of your child's skin.

• Check your pets for any signs of infection because they may also need treatment for ringworm.

eczema

Increasingly common in children, eczema can be triggered by a number of things, including stress, certain foods and environmental factors. It is closely associated with asthma and hay fever, and there may also be an inherited susceptibility. Choosing an holistic approach to treatment, which will take both internal and external factors into account, can be particularly helpful.

common symptoms

- Patches of rough, flaky, red skin, mainly on the face, armpits, elbows, hands and knees
- Patches of dry, scaly skin
- Intensely itchy skin, sometimes with noticeable scratch marks
- Blisters or cracks, sometimes bleeding
- Weeping sores, with either a thin watery or a crusty yellow discharge
- Disturbed sleep patterns

triggers & irritants

- House dust, animal fur, pollen
- Synthetic fabrics and harsh wools, some types of bedding
- Extreme temperatures, such as hot and sunny or dry, cold weather, and central heating
- Certain foods, such as wheat and dairy products, and eggs
- Household chemicals and fragranced products, such as soap, bubble bath, baby lotions, fabric conditioners and household cleaners
- Certain plants, such as primula, arnica and poison ivy

conventional treatment

The aim is usually to soothe the skin as rapidly as possible by applying a steroid cream containing hydrocortisone. Your doctor may also prescribe antibiotics if the skin is raw and there is a risk of infection. In severe cases, she may recommend 'wet wrapping', in which the skin is wrapped in a wet bandage after the cream has been applied. She will also look at your child's diet and may suggest eliminating some common allergens.

complementary treatments

aromatherapy

• One of the best ways to relieve itchy irritated skin is a soothing bath with essential oils, and children love the scent.

Add 1 tablespoonful of almond, jojoba or sunflower oil to your child's bath, together with 2–3 drops of either lavender or geranium essential oil.

Make a soothing oatmeal bath by putting a small quantity of organic oats into a muslin bag, together with a ½ teaspoonful of vegetable oil and a drop of lavender essential oil. Hang this over one of the taps as you run the bath.

For a skin-soothing cream, mix 120 ml (4 fl. oz) of calamine lotion with 2 drops of lavender or German chamomile essential oils.

ayurvedic medicine

Ayurveda is helpful in treating stress-related disorders such as eczema, and works by treating the patient as a whole. The practitioner will advise you about your child's diet, exercise, sleep and other lifestyle issues, with the emphasis on obtaining the right balance. She may also suggest techniques for cleansing his body of toxins.

nutritional therapy

There is a strong link between food allergy and eczema. Nutritionists usually advise avoiding the most common allergens, such as wheat and dairy products, eggs, peanuts, citrus fruits, artificial colourings and flavourings, and over-sugared foods. It may also be worth getting your child tested for food intolerance.

Vitamin A helps to keep the skin smooth, soft and healthy, so a deficiency can worsen the symptoms of eczema. So can a lack of zinc and essential fatty acids, which causes the skin to become dry and sensitive. Boost your child's intake of omega 3 oils, which are found in oily fish such as salmon and mackerel.

homeopathy

There are many effective remedies but it is always best to consult a qualified homeopath, who will take into account your child's case history before making a diagnosis and recommending a treatment. Sulphur is commonly used for all types of skin problems.

bach flower remedies

Dr Bach's Rescue Cream will relieve irritated and itchy skin. This multi-purpose skin salve contains a blend of six flower remedies to moisturize rough, dry skin and restore its natural condition. It can be used on the face, hands and body.

naturopathy

Viola tricolor, a fresh plant extract made from wild pansy, is especially effective. Try a cream made from extract of wild pansy. Drinking tea made from wild pansy is also thought to reinforce the skin's healing process. Bathing the affected area in warm whey is also a helpful treatment.

common sense

• Dress your child in loose, cotton clothing.

• Use pure cotton towels.

• Give him lukewarm baths.

• Consider giving him a supplement of Evening Primrose oil, thought to help.

• To soothe the irritation, soak a gauze pad in ice-cold milk and hold it against his skin for a few minutes.

nappy rash

This common and harmless rash affects most babies at some time or another, but they generally grow out of it after the first year. Nevertheless, severe nappy rash can be very distressing. It usually takes the form of irritant dermatitis and is triggered by a combination of exposure to urine and heat/friction from wearing a nappy. Occasionally, nappy rash can become infected with bacteria or a fungus. It tends to look worse than it is, but should always be treated. This can be done simply at home.

common symptoms

- Red spots or patches of inflamed skin, particularly where skin is in contact with the nappy
- Tight, shiny skin that may also become scaly
- A bright red rash around the anus
- Red patches spreading beyond the nappy area, for example, to the chest and back
- Red, irritated patches in the creases of the leg and groin
- A strong fishy odour when changing the nappy (caused by ammonia in the urine reacting to warmth)
- Itchiness and patches of inflamed skin elsewhere on the body (may indicate eczema)
- Pus-filled blisters and spots (sign of infection)

triggers & irritants

- Wearing wet or soiled nappies for long periods
- Over-heating
- Reaction to brand of nappy and/or washing powder
- Reaction to baby wipes or other cleansing agents, such as soap or baby lotion
- Change of diet – some babies develop nappy rash when they start on solids
- Certain foods – common triggers include citrus fruit, peas and raisins, which tend to pass straight through your baby's system
- Sensitive skin or proneness to allergies, such as eczema
- Antibiotic treatment – which may result in Candida, if the child also gets nappy rash
- Teething

conventional treatment

Nappy rash can usually be treated quickly and simply at home. Consult your health visitor or doctor if the rash does not improve after a couple of days or is spreading, or if your baby seems unwell.

Occasionally, nappy rash can lead to thrush (Candida). If you find any white patches inside your baby's mouth, these could indicate oral thrush (see page 67), so visit your doctor, who may prescribe an anti-fungal gel or liquid.

complementary treatments

aromatherapy

Helpful essential oils include chamomile, lavender, palmarosa and yarrow.

• Add 1–2 drops of German chamomile to a scoop of zinc oxide cream and apply it to the affected area.

• If your baby has thrush, add a couple of drops of tea tree oil to some natural yogurt and smooth over the patches.

• Rinse your baby's bottom with the following solution:

Add 4 drops each of German chamomile and lavender to 600 ml (1 pint) of boiling water, cover and leave to cool, then pour the mixture through a paper coffee filter.

• For a soothing bath, add 1 drop of German chamomile and 1 drop of lavender to a tablespoonful of whole milk. Add this to your baby's bath water. Make sure that it does not go in her eyes.

homeopathy

Calendula cream is excellent for soothing the stinging and burning sensation in mild cases of nappy rash.

Apis is useful for nappy rash that is hot, red and swollen, and aggravated by washing.

Cantharis can be used when the rash is severe and resembles a burn, and when urinating causes a painful, stinging sensation.

Rhus tox is for spots that are sore and raised, and that improve with regular bathing.

Sulphur can be used if the nappy rash is red, raw and bleeding.

western herbalism

Wash your baby's bottom with a herbal infusion of lavender, chamomile or marigold. Rose water, St John's wort oil and calendula oil are also helpful for nappy rash. Marigold cream can be used to protect and heal the skin.

common sense

• Dress your baby in loose-fitting clothing so air can circulate.

• Leave off her nappy whenever possible, especially during the warmer months.

• Change her nappies frequently.

• Try another brand of nappy to see if it suits your baby better.

• If you wash your baby's nappies, always use a non-biological powder designed for sensitive skins.

• Apply a good zinc oxide barrier cream to her bottom.

• Do not use soap and water or baby lotion on her bottom because it will sting.

• Avoid using talc, which can cake on the skin, holding in the damp.

• Apply egg white to the affected area of her bottom, drying it with a hair dryer on a cool setting. This will provide a protective layer that allows the skin to heal more quickly.

• Steer clear of any foods that might trigger or aggravate the condition.

urticaria (hives)

This is an allergic reaction that brings the child out in itchy red weals with white heads that look like nettle stings. It is caused by a sudden release of histamine in response to an irritant or allergen. Very common in children, a rash can appear after eating certain foods, such as nuts, eggs, strawberries, seafood and chocolate. The weals appear suddenly and usually fade within a couple of hours.

common symptoms

- Raised white spots or patches with a clear red edge, often circular
- A series of spots or a continuous area of inflamed skin that starts spreading
- Weals are usually very itchy, with a white or yellow lump in the middle
- Weals fade after a couple of hours but may flare up again, sometimes elsewhere
- Swelling around the rash, particularly on the face, that can last for days
- Sore eyes from rubbing
- Headache, listlessness, joint pains and feeling generally unwell

triggers & irritants

- Foods such as wheat and dairy products, eggs, citrus fruit, berries (especially strawberries), nuts, tomatoes, potatoes, chocolate and seafood
- Food additives and preservatives, such as tartrazine
- Salicylates (natural) — found in certain fruits (such as raisins), vegetables, herbs, cordials and fruit-flavoured drinks
- Salicylates (synthetic) – found in a variety of products, including medicines, perfumes and solvents
- House dust mite, animal fur and dander, pollen
- Certain plants, such as nettles, primula, arnica and poison ivy
- Bites and stings from insects, such as ants, midges, wasps or bees.
- Aspirin, penicillin, antibiotics and eye drops
- Sunlight
- Over-heating, perhaps from exercise
- Stress

Warning Occasionally the rash can spread to the throat and constrict the airways, causing wheezing and other breathing difficulties. If your child's face, mouth or tongue start to swell, contact your doctor immediately or take him to the emergency department of the nearest hospital. He may need a shot of adrenaline.

conventional treatment

If you think that you know what is causing the reaction, do not let your child come into contact with the allergen. Tell your doctor, who will be able to confirm your diagnosis. She may refer your child to hospital for allergy testing, a simple procedure that usually involves skin-prick tests, patch tests or sometimes blood tests. Generally antihistamines are prescribed to reduce the itching.

complementary treatments

aromatherapy

Urticaria is a very irritating condition and essential oils that bring relief include German chamomile, Roman chamomile, helichrysum and lavender.

• Try applying a soothing blend of the following to your child's bath:

Mix together 5 drops each of German chamomile and lavender, and add 2–3 drops to a warm bath. Adding half a cup of baking soda to the bath will also help.

• Add 4 drops each of lavender and German chamomile to 1 tablespoonful of calamine lotion and apply to the affected area to relieve itching.

homeopathy

Urtica urens is made from stinging nettles and is indicated when the rash looks like nettle stings. Urtica ointment or tincture will help soothe the irritation.

Rhus tox is made from poison ivy and helps if the rash has blistered.

Apis is made from bee venom and is used when the weals are red and swollen, perhaps with swelling under the eyes.

nutritional therapy

There is a strong link between food and skin allergies. The problem foods are often those that the child likes most. Try eliminating favourite foods for a while and see if the problem clears up. A nutritionist can help to identify the foods that may be causing your child problems. She will usually advise avoiding the most common allergens, such as wheat and dairy products, eggs, peanuts, citrus fruits, artificial colourings and flavourings, and over-sugared foods.

western herbalism

• To clear heat and congestion from your child's system, give cooling and cleansing herbs, such as burdock, rose and wild pansy, as teas three times a day. In extreme cases, give herbs to boost the immune system, such as chamomile and echinacea as well.

• Aloe vera gel applied to the skin is cooling and soothing. Even better, add a pinch of turmeric.

• Rose water is an excellent soother for inflamed skin.

common sense

• Try to identify the cause of your child's allergy so that you can prevent him coming in to contact with it.

• Try to remember what your child has just eaten. Keeping a food diary will help to track potential allergens.

• Apply a cold facecloth or ice pack to the affected areas.

• Keep your child out of the sun and encourage him to lie in a cool, darkened room until the worst symptoms have cleared up.

skin allergies

An allergic reaction is triggered when the body's immune system over-reacts to an allergen in the environment, such as pollen, animal fur and the house-dust mite, or certain foods. The skin is often the first part of the body to show an allergic reaction. Some children are prone to skin allergies, particularly if there is a family history of allergy. Certain allergies can affect anyone, for example contact dermatitis, which is a specific reaction to close contact with a particular substance, such as elastic. Skin rashes may also accompany an illness.

common symptoms

- An itchy, red, purple or pink rash, either as a series of spots or as a continuous area of inflamed skin
- Rough, flaky red patches on areas of skin that have been in contact with an allergen, such as a chemical (contact dermatitis)
- Dry, scaly red patches on the face and in the skin folds (eczema, see page 58)
- Itchy red patches, with a white head resembling nettle stings, all over the body (urticaria, see page 62)
- Headaches, dizziness and generally feeling unwell
- Rapid breathing and shortage of breath

triggers & irritants

- Synthetic fabrics, such as elastic
- Nickel
- House dust, animal fur, pollen
- Certain foods, such as wheat and dairy products, eggs, seafood, berries, chocolate
- Certain food additives, such as tartrazine, the synthetic yellow food colouring
- Household chemicals, such as soap, bubble bath, baby lotions, fabric conditioners, fragrance and household cleaners
- Sensitivity to certain plants, such as primula, arnica and poison ivy
- Medication, such as penicillin
- Bites and stings, for example from bees, wasps, ants and mosquitoes
- Emotional state – upheaval, stress and anxiety can all trigger skin problems

conventional treatment

If you know what is causing the reaction, do not let your child come into contact with that substance. Ask your doctor to confirm your diagnosis. He may refer your child to hospital for an allergy test. This is a simple procedure that usually involves skin-prick tests, patch tests or sometimes blood tests. Treatment generally includes antihistamines to reduce the itching and steroid creams to reduce the inflammation.

Warning Always take your child to the doctor if the rash is accompanied by fever, which could indicate an infection, or if the rash gets worse and spreads or does not improve after 48 hours.

complementary treatments

aromatherapy

One of the best ways to relieve an itchy, irritated skin is with a soothing bath.

Add 1 tablespoonful each of bicarbonate of soda and baking soda, plus 2 drops each of German chamomile and lavender essential oils to your child's bath and swish well into the water.

nutritional therapy

A nutritionist can help to identify the foods that are causing the problem, which can then be eliminated from your child's diet. There is a strong link between food and skin allergies. Nutritionists usually advise avoiding the most common allergens, such as wheat and dairy products, eggs, peanuts, citrus fruits, artificial colourings and flavourings, and over-sugared foods. The problem foods are often those that the child likes most. You could try eliminating favourite foods for a while to see if the problem clears up.

homeopathy

Allergies are a complex issue, so always consult a qualified homeopath. He will take your child's case history into account before making a diagnosis and recommending a remedy. Sulphur is useful for all types of skin problems.

kinesiology

This is particularly helpful in identifying allergies that may trigger other symptoms. The kinesiologist will test your child's muscles in order to identify areas of stress and blocked energy, and to isolate potential allergies. Once he has made a diagnosis, he will offer your child nutritional support.

herbalism

A cooled infusion of agrimony applied on a clean facecloth can help to soothe inflamed skin.

Add 5 dessertspoonsful of the dried plant to 250 ml (8 fl. oz) of cold water. Bring to the boil for 5 minutes, cool and strain. Apply four to five times a day.

common sense

• Breastfeeding will help to protect your child against allergies.

• Eliminate any common allergens, such as peanuts, eggs and dairy products, from your child's diet.

• Avoid using highly scented bath products and make sure that your household cleaners and washing powders do not contain harsh chemicals.

head lice

This is a common problem, particularly in children of nursery and primary school age. The lice make no distinction between clean and dirty, long or short, and curly or straight hair, and crawl rapidly from head to head when children sit close together. Although tiny, lice are still visible to the human eye. They like warmth and cling to the base of the hair shaft, where they suck blood from the scalp. They attach their almost invisible eggs to the hair shaft. Eggs hatch in about 7–10 days, leaving behind the empty eggshells, called nits.

common symptoms

- Itchy scalp, sometimes not for several weeks after infection
- White specks (nits) on the hair that resemble dandruff but cannot be easily brushed out
- Red, irritated scalp
- Red rash on the nape of the neck and behind the ears
- Swollen glands if the lice bites become infected

conventional treatment

Commercially available shampoos and insecticidal treatments are usually recommended, although head lice are gradually becoming resistant to many of these formulas and most should not be used on pre-school children. It is important to wet-comb your child's hair to remove the eggs and nits. The best option is to use a metal flea comb designed for pets, which has closely spaced teeth.

complementary treatments

homeopathy

Staphisagria can be used to prevent re-infestation, particularly if your child is distressed by the head lice.

aromatherapy

Essential oils are very effective, particularly anti-bacterial lavender and eucalyptus, deep-cleansing tea tree, and hair-friendly rosemary.

- Gently warm a few tablespoonsful of a carrier oil, such as sunflower or olive oil, then add 15 drops of lavender oil and a few drops each of rosemary and tea tree oils. Comb through your child's hair and leave, ideally overnight, then shampoo. Follow up with a tea tree conditioner.

- If your child's scalp has become irritated, add 1 drop of German chamomile and 2 drops of lavender oil to 1 teaspoonful of carrier oil and gently massage in with your fingertips.

- Add a few drops of lavender and tea tree oils to water in a plant spray and spritz on to your child's hair as a protective measure.

thrush (oral)

Common in babies and children, thrush is caused by a yeast infection called *Candida albicans*. This usually affects the mouth and throat, but can also affect the stomach and intestines. It usually responds well to complementary treatment.

common symptoms

- Itchy white patches inside the mouth and on the tongue and gums
- Refusal to eat

triggers & irritants

- Weakened immune system
- Antibiotics
- Asthma medication

conventional treatment

A doctor will prescribe anti-fungal liquids or gels, which you apply as drops to the sore patches in your child's mouth.

complementary therapies

homeopathy

Borax is the most common remedy for thrush in breastfeeding babies.

Sulphur can help if the mouth is red and burning.

Kali mur is indicated if the tongue is white.

nutritional therapy

Natural yogurt contains *Lactobacillus acidophilus* and is a well-known remedy for thrush. Give your child the unflavoured, unsweetened variety that contains 'friendly' bacteria. If your baby is weaned, avoid acidic food, such as fruit, which can aggravate the condition. If your child is older, eliminate sugar from his diet because thrush thrives on it. He should also avoid wheat and dairy products, and foods containing yeast.

common sense

- Wash your hands carefully after changing nappies.

- Make sure your child washes his hands before and after using the toilet.

- If you are breastfeeding, wash your nipples after each feed so you do not re-infect your baby.

- Apply natural yogurt to affected areas.

prickly heat

Also known as heat rash, this is very common in babies and young children. It develops as a result of the child's immature sweat glands over-reacting to heat and being unable to cool down her body efficiently. It tends to occur at the onset of hot weather or on first arriving in a hot climate. As the rash is aggravated by sweating, try to keep your child cool and out of the sun as much as possible.

common symptoms

- Rash of red or pink bumps that sometimes fill with fluid, developing into small blisters
- Affected areas tend to be parts of the body that sweat the most or are exposed to sunlight – face, neck and shoulders, armpits and groin, trunk.
- Hot, pink cheeks
- Restlessness and irritability

triggers & irritants

- Strong sunlight and hot weather
- Over-heating caused by wearing too much clothing in hot weather or sleeping in a stuffy room
- Fair-skinned children are more prone to developing prickly heat than dark-skinned children

conventional treatment

Calamine is supposed to help but makes the condition worse because it blocks the pores, trapping sweat and allowing heat to build up. If the rash is still obvious after several hours, even though your child has cooled down, contact your doctor. If the rash persists and your child develops other symptoms, such as vomiting or headaches, or seems generally unwell, seek medical help.

complementary treatments

aromatherapy

Essential oils that can help include lavender, Roman chamomile and eucalyptus.

Mix 2 tablespoons of baking soda with 2–3 drops of lavender essential oil and add to a warm bath.

homeopathy

Sol is a good all-round remedy for dealing with the side-effects of too much sun. It can also be used to treat prickly heat and to prevent sunburn in children with fair skin.

western herbalism

• Make a cooling rinse for the skin by adding burdock, chamomile or marigold flowers to a jug of cool water and using as necessary to soothe and comfort.

• Aloe vera gel is cooling and soothing, and should be applied liberally to the skin to bring relief.

• Rosewater and witch hazel are cooling and soothing lotions.

traditional chinese medicine

Prickly heat can be related to a child's inability to cope with extra heat because of excess internal heat. Eliminating 'heating' foods, such as garlic, onions, spices, cheese and yogurt, from the diet is thought to help.

common sense

• If your child's room is too hot – it should be between 16 and 20°C (60 and 68°F) – adjust the heating or open a window. An electric fan may bring short-term relief.

• Give your child a cooling bath, in water just above body temperature, or wipe her down with a sponge or facecloth.

• Offer your child plenty of drinks, preferably water or diluted fruit juice – to keep her fluid levels up.

• Keep your child's skin as dry as possible.

• Avoid using calamine lotion, which will cake on the skin, causing a build-up of sweat. Also avoid mineral-based sun creams that might block the pores.

• Dress your child in cool, loose-fitting cotton clothing, such as a baggy T-shirt, so that as much of her skin as possible is exposed to the air. Avoid clothing made from artificial fibres.

• Protect your child from strong sunlight, dressing her appropriately during hot, dry weather conditions.

• Avoid scented products, such as soaps or bubble baths, until the rash has gone.

• Consider changing your washing powder, because some brands contain ingredients that may aggravate skin conditions.

cradle cap

This scalp condition, common in babies and sometimes young children, doesn't look very nice but is harmless. It is caused by over-production of sebum, the oily substance produced by the skin's sebaceous glands. This leads to the build-up of a greasy crust on the scalp. Occasionally cradle cap can spread to other areas, when it becomes known as seborrhoeic dermatitis. It can also be a precursor to eczema.

common symptoms

- Cradle cap usually covers the soft areas of a baby's head (the fontanelles)
- A build-up of dead skin
- Dry, scaly, sometimes crusty patches on the scalp, turning yellow, orange or dark brown
- Flaky skin spreads to the forehead, behind the ears and occasionally around the eyebrows; more rarely, it affects the skin fold of the thighs (seborrhoeic dermatitis)
- Scales may smell, due to the build-up of pus underneath

triggers & irritants

- Over-heating and sweating of the scalp
- Over-production of sebum

conventional treatment

Special shampoos for cradle cap are available from pharmacies, but these may irritate your child's skin further. If the cradle cap is very stubborn, your doctor may suggest a mild hydrocortisone cream because of the risk of infection. A build-up of scales on the scalp can be caused by several other conditions, including ringworm, psoriasis and eczema, so consult your doctor if you have any doubts.

complementary treatments

aromatherapy

Tea tree, geranium, lemon and orange essential oils can help.

Mix 1 tablespoonful each of avocado oil and jojoba oil with 1 drop each of tea tree, orange and lemon essential oils. Smooth a small amount gently over your child's scalp, leave for a few minutes then use a mild shampoo to cleanse the hair. Be careful that none of the oil gets into his eyes.

homeopathy

If the cradle cap is sore, itchy or causing your child distress, use a gentle Calendula cream. If the cradle cap is severe, think about consulting a qualified homeopath for constitutional treatment.

nutritional therapy

This condition is thought to be caused by a deficiency of essential fatty acids and/or zinc during pregnancy. Make sure your child's diet is ritch in essential fatty acids by including plenty of oily fish, which is helpful in treating dermatitis.

herbalism

After shampooing, rinse the hair with a burdock infusion by soaking 1 teaspoonful of dried burdock in a cup of boiling water. Leave to cool before using. You can also use ordinary tea.

naturopathy

Rubbing St John's wort oil, traditionally used to treat skin irritations, or diluted cider vinegar into the scalp usually helps.

common sense

• Keep your child's head uncovered and exposed to the fresh air whenever possible.

• Never pick off the crusts or rub the scalp vigorously, as this can cause soreness and bleeding, which in turn leads to infection. Loose flaky areas can be removed with a soft brush, but the condition is best left alone.

• Rub a small amount of warmed olive oil or sunflower oil, preferably cold pressed and organic, into your child's scalp to loosen the scales. Leave overnight (protect pillows with a soft towel) and wash out with a mild shampoo in the morning. Towel dry his hair and use a soft bristle brush to gently lift out any loose flakes. Repeat as often as needed until the condition of the scalp has improved.

chickenpox

This highly infectious viral disease can be caught only by close contact with an infected person. Children of all ages, but more usually those under the age of 10 years, can get chickenpox. The disease is spread either by droplets of saliva or in the fluid that oozes from the blisters. It takes between 10 and 21 days to incubate, and the child is most infectious from a couple of days before the rash appears until scabs have formed on the blisters.

common symptoms

- Headache, sore throat and general malaise
- Raised temperature and mild fever
- Loss of appetite
- Swollen lymph glands
- Rash of small red spots on the scalp and face, spreading to the rest of the body, particularly the stomach and back, and possibly even inside the mouth and ears
- Spots rapidly develop into intensely itchy blisters, which form itchy yellow scabs that eventually drop off

conventional treatment

Once diagnosis has been confirmed you can usually treat the infection yourself at home. If your child's temperature is raised, give her children's paracetamol and take measures to soothe the irritation.

complementary treatments

aromatherapy

- Essential oils that can help include lavender, Roman chamomile and German chamomile.

Add 10 drops of German chamomile and 30 drops of lavender essential oil to a bottle of calamine lotion. Shake well to mix then apply to the affected skin.

- Make a soothing oatmeal bath for your child: wrap a handful of oatmeal in a piece of material such as muslin, adding 4 drops of German chamomile and 4 drops of lavender essential oils. Tie the bag around the bath tap so that the water can run through it.

homeopathy

Rhus tox is the best-known remedy for chickenpox and is particularly helpful in soothing the itching.

Ant tart helps when the spots develop into larger blisters and your child is miserable.

western herbalism

- An echinacea supplement will help speed recovery by boosting the immune system. Garlic and tumeric are also helpful. Add a ¼ teaspoonful of tumeric to dishes, or give your child garlic capsules.

- Chamomile tea will relieve itching.

- An infusion of burdock and peppermint added to the bath water helps soothe irritated skin.

boils

Affecting children of all ages, a boil is a skin infection that results in a hard, pus-filled lump under the surface of the skin. It is very tender and painful, and usually appears on the face, neck, buttocks, back, armpits or groin. It can be very distressing for a child, particularly if it is noticeable.

common symptoms

- A hard, sore lump under the surface of the skin
- Soreness around the affected area
- Swollen glands

triggers & irritants

- Infected hair follicle
- Infected sebaceous gland
- Lowered resistance to infection
- Feeling run down
- Poor diet and too much fatty food
- Constipation
- Lack of exercise
- Diabetes

conventional treatment

Boils usually burst of their own accord. Sometimes they need lancing, which should always be carried out by a doctor. If the boil does not come to a head after 2–3 days, seek medical advice.

complementary treatments

aromatherapy

To draw out the pus, put a drop of antiseptic thyme essential oil on to a hot compress and hold it against the boil twice a day. Once it has burst, dab on a mix of anti-bacterial lavender and tea tree oils.

homeopathy

Hepar sulph is helpful when pus has formed and the boil is tender to the touch.

Belladonna can be applied in the early stages of a boil, when it is red and angry.

bach flower remedies

Crab Apple will help to cleanse the area and detoxify your child's body.

western herbalism

- Apply equal parts of honey and cod liver oil as a fresh compress daily.

- Bake an onion in the oven and use as a hot poultice daily.

- Give your child echinacea to cleanse her system and reduce the infection.

common sense

- Add Epsom salts and sea salt to the water when washing the affected area to prevent infection spreading.

- Do not squeeze boils – they will eventually come to a head on their own.

ear ache, ear infections & glue ear

Ear ache and infections are common in young children, who tend to have narrow Eustachian tubes (the drainage canals running from the ear to the nose and throat). As a result, if a child has a cold, the mucus cannot drain away, which can cause ear ache and hearing problems. Occasionally the middle ear can become infected. Glue ear is a common condition where the middle ear fills up with a thick discharge that leads to hearing difficulties.

common symptoms

• Pain in the ear

• Pulling or rubbing the ears

• Discharge from the ear

• Loss of hearing on the affected side

• Swollen glands and tonsils

• Raised temperature

• Crying

• Dizziness (in older children)

triggers & irritants

• Colds (mild ear ache)

• Tonsillitis, sinusitis, hay fever, sore throats, coughs and colds (middle ear infections)

• Upper respiratory tract infections (glue ear)

• Antibiotics – which can suppress symptoms and result in recurrent infection

• Toothache

• Spots and boils in or near the ear

• Very cold weather, wind and snow

• Cigarette smoke

• Changes in cabin pressure when flying

conventional treatment

If you suspect that your child has an ear infection, consult your doctor immediately because in some cases it can lead to a perforated eardrum. Also consult your doctor if the pain continues for more than 24 hours or your child suffers any loss of hearing.

Doctors tend to treat ear aches and ear infections with painkillers and antibiotics. This can lead to a cycle of re-infection that may result in a ruptured eardrum or catarrhal deafness (glue ear). The conventional treatment for glue ear is antibiotics or an operation to insert grommets into the eardrum in order to drain the fluid.

complementary treatments

aromatherapy

The best oils to use include lemon, neem, eucalyptus, lavender, thyme linalol or chamomile.

• Make a massage mixture by adding 1 drop each of lavender and thyme linalol essential oils to 1 teaspoonful of olive oil and gently rub it into the skin around the ears, neck and throat.

• Apply a hot compress directly to the ear to bring relief. Use a cloth wrung out in hot water to which a few drops of lavender or thyme linalol essential oil have been added.

homeopathy

Aconite is prescribed for sudden intense ear ache, often caused by extreme weather conditions.

Belladonna is offered for sudden inflammation, where the face is red and there is also a fever.

Chamomilla is the remedy for acute ear ache when your child is crying with pain.

Hepar sulph is used for ear infections accompanied by thick yellow catarrh.

western herbalism

• Give your child one garlic perle every 2 hours while the pain is acute. Include garlic in his diet as a preventive measure.

• Offer him plenty of hot drinks, such as lemon and honey, blackcurrant juice or herbal teas.

• Boosting your child's immune system can help as a preventive. Use mild spices, such as coriander, ginger, turmeric and cardamon in your cooking.

nutritional therapy

Nutritional therapists believe that glue ear is often linked to food allergy. If you suspect that a particular food may be causing your child's problem, keep a food diary, then consult a therapist who can help you to identify the allergy and advise on a special elimination diet.

acupuncture

This can be of great benefit if the underlying cause is a disharmony that is disturbing your child's *chi*.

common sense

• Hold a covered hot-water bottle against your child's ear, as warmth can help to soothe ear ache.

• Do not give him solid food or dairy produce until the condition has cleared, but make sure that he has plenty of hot drinks.

• Avoid washing your child's hair at this time, but, if you must, cover his ears to prevent water getting in.

• Flying can aggravate ear ache. Swallowing can help – give your child something to suck or chew, particularly during take-off and landing.

sinusitis

Inflammation of the lining of the sinuses, known as sinusitis, produces a range of symptoms. Children usually develop it as the result of a cold or other respiratory tract infection, hay fever or allergy. It is more common in older children because babies and toddlers have relatively under-developed sinuses.

symptoms

- Blocked or runny nose
- Bad breath
- Loss of sense of smell
- Pain and puffiness around the eyes
- Headaches
- Build-up of pressure in the head

triggers & irritants

- Upper respiratory tract infections, such as colds, influenza or coughs
- Allergies, such as allergic rhinitis or hay fever
- Tooth abscess
- Injury to the nose
- Nasal polyps – breathing through the mouth because nose is blocked

conventional treatment

Decongestants and nasal sprays ease the symptoms, and saline sprays are also widely used. A doctor will usually prescribe antibiotics if your child has an infection. In more severe cases the doctor may recommend draining the sinuses.

complementary treatments

aromatherapy

Add 4 drops of rosemary, 2 drops of eucalyptus and 6 drops of ravensura essential oils to a bowl containing 600 ml (20 fl. oz) of warm water. Dip a facecloth into the water and place it on your child's forehead to soothe the congestion.

Add 4 drops of ravensara, 4 drops of niaouli and 4 drops of Roman chamomile essential oils to a bowl of steaming water and place in your child's bedroom.

nutritional approaches

Nutritionists attribute many cases of sinusitis to food allergy. At the first sign of infection, exclude all dairy products from your child's diet and cut down on wheat, both of which are thought to boost mucus production. Make sure that she eats plenty of fresh fruit and vegetables. You could also give her a supplement of vitamin C.

naturopathy

Cutting down on mucus-forming foods and eliminating salt from the diet can help, plus a supplement of garlic perles and herbal support. Echinacea helps to boost the immune system.

natural common sense

- Run a very hot bath and sit your child in the bathroom – not the bath – to inhale the steam.

halitosis

Younger children occasionally suffer from bad breath, which is usually caused by bacterial activity in the mouth due to infection or poor dental hygiene. It is usually most noticeable when they have a cold.

common symptoms

- **Unpleasant mouth odour**
- **Breath smells like rotting eggs**

triggers & irritants

- **An empty stomach**
- **Constipation**
- **Infection of the tonsils, nose or mouth**
- **Catarrh**
- **A cold**
- **Poor tooth-brushing**
- **Diabetes – a smell of acetone (nail-varnish remover)**
- **Appendicitis – a generally foul smell**
- **Gum disease**
- **Tooth decay**

conventional treatment

Bad breath on its own is not usually a sufficient reason to take your child to the doctor. Make an appointment to see your dentist, because gum disease or tooth decay might be causing the problem.

complementary treatments

aromatherapy

Try a toothpaste containing tea tree or eucalyptus essential oil and supervise teeth brushing.

traditional chinese medicine

Bad breath is usually treated as a dysfunction of the stomach. Taste in the mouth can indicate a variety of possible disharmonies, usually of the spleen and stomach but sometimes also of the kidneys and liver.

nutritional therapy

Bad breath is often a result of constipation. Toxins from the bowel are absorbed into the bloodstream and released in the breath. Give your child a fibre-rich diet that includes plenty of fresh fruit and vegetables and wholegrains, such as brown rice and oats, and make sure that she drinks plenty of water.

Another cause of bad breath is poor digestion, which leaves food fermenting in the stomach. Make sure that mealtimes are relaxed affairs and that your child chews her food well.

western herbalism

To prevent gum infection, add a few drops of echinacea tincture to a little water. Encourage your child to swill the liquid around their mouth then swallow.

styes

Styes are a bacterial infection that develops at the root of an eyelash, producing a small inflamed lump, rather like a small boil. This causes redness and swelling of the eyelid, so that the eye appears slightly closed. Styes often fill with pus and may burst. They are easily spread from one eye to the other.

common symptoms

- Itchiness, soreness and swelling of the eyelid.
- A painful red lump that develops a yellow head
- Inflammation along the rim of the eyelid
- Sensation of having something in the eye

triggers & irritants

- Bacterial infection
- Being run down
- Depressed immune system
- Natural susceptibility

conventional treatment

See your doctor if your child has a stye that is particularly large or painful, or if he tends to get them repeatedly. She can take swabs to locate the source of the infection. Also consult your doctor if a stye seems to have developed on the inside of the eyelid or if the pain persists.

complementary treatments

homeopathy

Hypercal Try a hot compress of a Hypercal solution three to four times a day. This should help to bring the stye to a head and prevent infection.

Pulsatilla is the best-known remedy, particularly if the stye is filled with pus.

nutritional therapy

If your child is run down, he may be prone to styes. Make sure that he eats plenty of fresh fruit and vegetables to boost his immune system.

western herbalism

Euphrasia is a well-established remedy for sore eyes. It is used in tinctures, infusions and eye lotions, and a compress is the most effective method for soothing a stye. Proprietary products are available but consult a herbalist first as these should be used only under medical supervision.

natural common sense

- Make sure that your child washes his hands frequently.
- Rinse a cotton-wool pad in hot water and hold over the stye.

conjunctivitis

Conjunctivitis is an inflammation of the membrane that covers the eyeball. If this affects the whole eye, it is probably due to a bacterial or viral infection. If your child has recurrent attacks, this may be due to an allergic reaction so it is important to isolate the trigger.

common symptoms

- Pink or red, bloodshot eyes
- Sore, irritated eyes that feel gritty or sandy
- Swollen eyelids
- Thin, watery discharge from the eyes
- Thick, sticky, yellow discharge that causes crustiness and sticks the eyelashes together
- Rubbing the eyes
- Impaired vision

triggers & irritants

- Bacterial or viral infection
- Allergy or hay fever
- Dirt and dust
- Environmental pollution
- Wind
- Foreign body, such as grit, in the eye
- Food intolerance, for example to dairy products
- Chlorine in swimming pools

conventional treatment

Your doctor will prescribe antibiotic drops or ointment. To clean your child's eyes, use cotton wool dipped in cooled, boiled water, wiping from the inner corner outwards and using a separate piece of cotton wool for each eye.

complementary treatments

homeopathy

Euphrasia is one of the best-known remedies, prescribed when the eyes are red and feeling gritty. It can be used both externally and internally.

Add 10 drops of Euphrasia tincture to 300 ml (10 fl. oz) of water, and bathe the eyes four times a day.

Pulsatilla is the remedy to use when there is a lot of thick yellow discharge.

bach flower remedies

A solution of Crab Apple can be used to bathe the eyes.

western herbalism

- Bathe the eyes three times a day with a tincture of rosewater.

Use 5 drops of rosewater and 5 drops of euphrasia mother tincture in half a cupful of warm sterilized water.

- Use a herbal compress.

Soak chamomile or fennel teabags in boiling water, remove when lukewarm and then place over each eye for 10 minutes as a soother.

chinese herbalism

According to this philosophy, the eyes are linked to the liver. Treatment involves the topical application of herbs and taking herbs internally for reinforcement. It works well when combined with acupuncture.

sore throat

A sore throat is an inflammation of the pharynx, also known as pharyngitis, and is usually caused by either a virus or a bacteria. Sore throats are common all year round, not just in the winter, and generally last for a day or two. Children often get sore throats as they accompany a cold, ear ache and flu, and usually clear up once the worst of the illness passes.

common symptoms

- **Painful throat**
- **Swollen tonsils, sometimes with white spots**
- **Difficulty in swallowing**
- **Fever**
- **Redness of the back of the mouth**
- **Bad breath**
- **Refusal to eat**
- **Feeling generally unwell**

triggers & irritants

- **Upper respiratory tract infection, such as a cold or cough**
- **Laryngitis**
- **Tonsillitis**
- **Scarlet fever**
- **Central heating**
- **Smoky atmospheres**

conventional treatment

Check your child's temperature and see if her glands are swollen by gently running your fingers down her neck – you may find small swellings that feel like peas. Some doctors prescribe antibiotics for bacterial infections, while others recommend paracetamol for pain relief.

complementary treatments

aromatherapy

Antiseptic oils, such as rosemary, thyme, lemon and eucalyptus, can be used as inhalations or to disinfect the room. Simply add a few drops to a water spray.

homeopathy

Aconite is helpful when a sore throat is accompanied by fever.

Hepar sulph is prescribed when the sore throat is very painful and may extend to the ears.

chiropractic

Children who experience recurrent sore throats often benefit from chiropractic treatment because they may have a restriction in the functioning of the neck. Chiropractic will also help to boost their immune system.

nutritional therapy

A nutritional therapist will recommend foods that strengthen the immune system and may also suggest supplements of vitamin C.

western herbalism

- Mix a chopped onion with a couple of dessertspoonsful of honey and leave for 30 minutes. Strain off the liquid and give your child a teaspoonful at regular intervals.

- Echinacea will boost the immune system against further infection.

tonsilitis

Inflammation of the tonsils is usually caused by streptococcal bacteria but may occasionally be caused by a virus. The tonsils become enlarged when fighting infection. It tends to be more common in children once they go to school. If your child suffers from recurrent tonsilitis, it is important to establish the cause so that it can be resolved.

common symptoms

- Red, swollen tonsils
- Swollen glands
- Sore throat
- Difficulty in swallowing
- Fever and chills
- Swollen adenoids, resulting in snoring
- Poor appetite and lethargy
- Cough
- Ear ache

triggers & irritants

- Viral or bacterial infections, such as colds, flu or laryngitis
- Congestion or catarrh
- Allergic reactions
- Being run down – lack of fresh air and exercise, poor diet
- Over-load of toxins in the system
- Smoky atmospheres
- Over-use of antibiotics

conventional treatment

Paracetamol can help with fever and pain. Take your child's temperature and check to see if her tonsils are infected by holding down her tongue with a spoon.

Always consult your doctor if your child has a fever with a sore throat and swollen glands. The standard treatment is a course of antibiotics. Tonsillectomy is still used to treat acute and recurrent tonsillitis, particularly if it is linked with breathing problems.

complementary treatments

aromatherapy

Add 3 drops of ginger and 5 drops of lemon essential oils to 2 tablespoonful of spring water, then add 3 tablespoonful of cider vinegar. Pour through a paper coffee filter, then add 1 tablespoonful of organic honey. Add 1 teaspoonful to a small glass of warm water and use as a gargle twice a day.

homeopathy

Belladonna is the remedy for the initial stages of tonsillitis and is often the only one needed. It helps with the sore throat and swelling.

western herbalism

- Echinacea, garlic and thyme are among the herbs that help the immune system.

- Dissolve ½ teaspoonful each of turmeric and salt in a cup of hot water and use as a gargle.

nutritional therapy

Give your child plenty of fresh fruit and vegetables to make sure that she is getting enough vitamin C to be able to fight the infection.

nose bleeds

Nose bleeds are a common problem and can occur at any age. Neverthless, they can be quite alarming, especially for small children. Nose bleeds are also common in children who are suffering from a cold or congestion because frequent or violent nose-blowing can damage the delicate lining of the nose. Always seek medical advice if a nose bleed follows a blow to the head.

triggers & irritants

- **Bumps or knocks to the nose**
- **Poking fingers or small objects up the nose**
- **Blowing the nose too hard**
- **Blow to the head**
- **Colds and other forms of congestion**

conventional treatments

Gently pinch your child's nose on the fleshy part just beneath the bridge. If the bleeding does not stop after 30 minutes, seek medical advice, especially if the nose bleed followed an injury.

If you are worried about nose bleeds in general, for example if they occur frequently with no obvious cause, consult your doctor, who may refer your child to a specialist. The problem may be a fragile blood vessel, which can be cauterized – a simple procedure that involves sealing it with heat.

complementary treatments

homeopathy

Arnica can be used for any nose bleed that follows an injury to the nose.

Phosphorus is used for bleeding triggered by frequent nose-blowing.

nutritional therapy

Vitamin C and bioflavonoids, which are found in fruit and vegetables such as peppers, watercress, broccoli and citrus, will help to strengthen the walls of the capillaries in the nose and prevent frequent nose bleeds. Weakening of the blood vessel walls can lead to an increase in nose bleeds.

natural common sense

- Do not insert anything into your child's nose to try to stem the bleeding.

- Get your child to sit down and lean forward, with his head over a basin or towel. Do not tip his head back. Encourage him to sit still and not to sniff.

- If the bleeding does not stop, apply a cold compress, such as a small pack of frozen peas.

- Soak some cotton wool balls in distilled witch hazel and hold them to his nose.

cold sores

Cold sores are small blisters that usually appear around the mouth and nostrils. They are caused by a virus which, once caught, will lie dormant and can be a recurring problem triggered by extreme cold and bright sunlight. The first sign is a tingling sensation, followed by the formation of a blister, which can be very sore and itchy. This will crust over after a few days and eventually heal.

common symptoms

- **Tingling sensation**
- **Small blisters around or on the lips, inside the mouth, around the nostrils and sometimes elsewhere on the face**

triggers & irritants

- **Existing infection with the virus**
- **Weak immune system/Being run down**
- **Kissing an infected person or sharing cups and other utensils**
- **Poor diet**
- **Cold or influenza**
- **Chickenpox and measles**
- **Physical or emotional stress**
- **Extreme temperatures and sunlight**

conventional treatment

Apply cold sore cream, lotion or petroleum jelly to the affected area at the first sign of tingling. If your child suffers from recurrent cold sores, consult your doctor. If the cold sore becomes infected, antibiotics will usually be prescribed.

complementary treatments

aromatherapy

Tea tree has anti-bacterial and anti-fungal properties. Apply neat or diluted in oil.

Mix 1 drop of lavender and tea tree essential oils with 1 drop of surgical spirit to help dry up the cold sores.

homeopathy

Rhus tox is indicated for cold sores that blister with pus.

Nat mur is helpful for cold sores triggered by sun.

nutritional therapy

- Vitamins A and E and zinc supplements are beneficial. Vitamin E oil can be applied directly to the cold sore.

- Lysine, an amino acid found in beans, chicken, lamb, and fresh fruit and vegetables, can help to prevent the virus from spreading.

- Arginine, an amino acid found in chocolate, coconut, peanuts, oats and wheat, should be avoided.

western herbalism

- Use calendula or tea tree cream to relieve the itching and soreness.

- Aloe vera gel is cooling and soothing. Apply it three times a day.

- Boost his immune system with an echinacea supplement.

teething

Babies usually start producing teeth from the age of about 5 months up to about 2 years. While some lucky children seem to be untroubled by teething, many others suffer a great deal. Parents tend to attribute many of their baby's minor upsets to teething. Give your baby lots of tender loving care – cuddles are the best form of reassurance.

common symptoms

- Gum inflammation
- Dribbling
- Rash around the mouth
- Biting on anything
- Putting fist in mouth
- Crying and irritability, fretful behaviour
- Red cheek on the affected side
- Clinginess
- Disturbed sleep
- Catarrh and colds
- Fever
- Tummy upset and diarrhoea
- Nappy rash

triggers & irritants

- Eruption of a tooth, which pierces the gum, causing inflammation and pain

conventional treatment

Rubbing teething gel on the gums has a numbing effect. Consult you doctor if your child develops a fever that lasts longer than 2 days because she may have an unrelated infection.

complementary treatments

aromatherapy

Make up a soothing mix to help your baby sleep.

Add 1 drop of petitgrain and 1 drop of lavender essential oils to a tablespoonful of vegetable oil and gently rub this into your baby's back.

homeopathy

Chamomilla is the most common remedy for teething where one cheek is red and the child is irritable and has diarrhoea. Homeopathic chamomile teething granules may also help.

Belladonna can be used if there is a fever and the child is burning hot.

Pulsatilla is good for children who are clingy and miserable.

bach flower remedies

Rescue Remedy diluted in cooled, boiled water can be rubbed on to the gums or given orally. This will help to calm a distressed baby.

natural common sense

- Give your child something hard to bite on, such as a piece of carrot or apple.
- Cold yogurt is a great soother.
- Gently massage the sore gum with your fingertip.
- Offer her plenty of drinks of cooled, boiled water.

catarrh

Too much mucus in the nose and throat is known as catarrh. This is caused by the mucus membrane becoming inflamed and producing too much mucus. As a result, the child suffers from congestion and becomes snuffly, with a runny nose, cough and even ear ache. Catarrh tends to be particularly common in pre-schoolers but children often grow out of it, usually by the time they go to secondary school.

common symptoms

- Congestion
- Runny nose
- Cough
- Ear ache
- Muffled breathing

triggers

- Upper respiratory tract infections, such as a cold, influenza or cough
- Allergy, such as allergic rhinitis or hay fever
- Sinusitis
- Enlarged adenoids
- Ear ache/ear infections
- Nasal polyps – breathing through the mouth because the nose is blocked

conventional treatment

Unless you think an allergy or infection is causing the catarrh, it is not necessary to seek medical advice. Doctors usually prescribe nose drops if there is an accompanying loss of appetite, with decongestants for use at night.

complementary treatments

aromatherapy

- Eucalyptus, ravensara and frankincense essential oils can help.

Add 3 drops of ravensara and 1 drop of eucalyptus to 1 teaspoonful of vegetable oil, and rub into his chest before bedtime.

- Lavender or tea tree essentials oils burned in a diffuser will help ease the symptoms of snuffly children.

nutritional therapy

Give your child plenty of fresh fruit and vegetables to boost her immune system. Consider giving her a supplement of vitamin C and zinc, and avoid dairy products, which can accelerate mucus production. Cutting salt out of the child's diet is also believed to help.

naturopathy

- To stop a runny nose, dip a slice of fresh onion into a cup of hot water and persuade your child to drink it.

- Echinacea is recommended for catarrh.

traditional chinese medicine

Garlic is recommended for this complaint. It is not very popular with children, but it can be taken in capsule form, with none of the taste or smell.

asthma

Asthma is on the increase and now affects one in seven children. Irritation results in swelling of the tubes that carry air to the lungs (the bronchioles). This obstructs the flow of air, causing wheezing and breathing problems. The severity of asthma varies – in some cases it can even be life-threatening – and it is a condition that needs medication. Complementary therapies can help as part of an integrated approach.

common symptoms

- Wheezing and gasping
- Dry, irritating, persistent cough
- Night-time cough
- Difficulty shifting coughs and colds
- Pain or tightness in the chest

triggers & irritants

- Pet fur, saliva, and feathers
- Mites in house dust
- Respiratory infections, such as coughs and colds, and hay fever
- Certain foods and preservatives
- Household cleaners and other fragranced products
- Predisposition to allergies
- Environmental pollutants, such as car fumes and cigarette smoke
- Cold air and foggy atmospheres
- Emotional factors: stress and anxiety

conventional treatments

Diagnosis of asthma is with a peak-flow monitor, which shows the rate at which air can be forced out of the lungs. Most children are able to control their asthma with inhalers. Younger children may need an attachment, known as a spacer, to enable them to inhale the medication correctly. There are two methods of medication inhalation:

- Bronchodilators are reliever inhalers and are used for asthma flare-ups, for example before a sports activity.

- Preventer inhalers are used daily by children with permanent asthma, even when they appear well.
Both methods work by reducing the inflammation of the airways.

complementary treatments

aromatherapy

To reduce stress, give your child a soothing bath.

Add 10 drops of Roman chamomile, 8 drops of mandarin and 2 drops of geranium essential oils to 4 tablespoonsful of carrier oil. Add ¼ tsp (under 4 years); ½ tsp (5–8 years); 1 tsp (8–12 years) to your child's bathwater.

homeopathy

Asthma requires constitutional treatment, so consult a qualified practitioner in conjunction with your doctor.

massage therapy

Back massage can help. Gently massage over your child's entire back, using large upward-sweeping movements.

nutritional therapy

Asthma is a sign that your child's immune system is compromised, so it can be helpful to identify and eliminate any potential food allergens in his diet. The most common allergens are dairy products, eggs, nuts and oranges, and artificial colourings, flavourings and preservatives. If your child has a marked fondness for a particular food, and eats it every day, this is probably the first item to cut out.

An asthma prevention diet includes plenty of fresh fruit and vegetables, which have been shown to have positive benefits to lung health. It also eliminates dairy produce, which can lead to excess mucus production, so try to cut out or reduce these wherever possible. Wheat and other grains can also be a trigger. Changing to organic produce may help, as your child will not be exposed to so many pesticides. It is also important to cut down on fast food and fizzy drinks.

herbalism

Visit a medical herbalist who will give you support and advice on how to treat your child's asthma.

• Licorice is a great remedy for asthma. It is soothing and can really help an attack of wheezing. Give your child a cup of licorice tea to sip. Prepare by steeping a teaspoonful of licorice root in a cup of boiled water for 5 minutes.

• Echinacea, chamomile, garlic, cinnamon, ginger and turmeric are all herbs that support the immune system.

• Hot lemon and honey drinks can help clear mucus. (Honey should not be given to children younger than 12 months.)

• Add 1 teaspoonful of cider vinegar to a cup of warm water sweetened with honey. Give this to your child to sip during wheezing attacks.

alexander technique

Breathing is an important aspect of the Alexander technique, which works by re-educating the body so that we stand and move correctly. This has health benefits because bad posture often leads to other symptoms, such as poor breathing caused by restrictions in the throat and diaphragm.

bach flower remedies

If emotional issues are causing your child's asthma problems, Rescue Remedy or Rock Rose can help to relieve stress and panic, and calm your child.

relaxation

Incorrect breathing can aggravate asthma. Practise regular deep breathing exercises with your child to help improve his lung function.

Your child should breathe in slowly so that his stomach expands outwards. He should then breathe out as slowly as possible, shaping his mouth as if he were going to whistle, breathing in for 3 seconds and out for 3 seconds.

kinesiology

This can help to identify any underlying allergies that may be triggering the asthma attacks, such as a food intolerance. The kinesiologist can then recommend a nutritional plan and further treatment.

acupuncture

This benefits children with asthma, especially when combined with Chinese herbs, diet and breathing exercises.

common sense

• Reduce your child's exposure to allergens: keep pets out of bedrooms, vacuum regularly and dust every day with a damp cloth.

• Avoid feather-filled pillows and duvets, instead opting for synthetic fibres.

• Invest in special protective mattress and pillow covers.

• Try putting soft toys in the freezer overnight to reduce exposure to house-dust mites.

• Try to avoid walking your child along busy main roads.

• Never allow anyone to smoke near your child or expose him to smoky atmospheres.

bronchitis

Bronchitis is a chest infection, triggered by a virus or bacteria, that leads to inflammation of the airways. It tends to affect toddlers and older children rather than babies. It often develops from a cold, spreading through the airways (bronchioles), which become inflamed and swollen. It usually takes a couple of weeks to get over an attack. Children often experience recurrent attacks of bronchitis. If you are worried, ask your doctor to refer your child to a specialist as there may be an underlying cause, such as asthma.

common symptoms

- Runny nose, sore throat and other influenza-like symptoms in the upper respiratory tract
- Dry, hacking cough, developing into a sore, chesty rattle, often much worse at night
- White or yellow phlegm
- Rapid breathing, often accompanied by wheezing and chest pain
- Flushed face, raised temperature and other symptoms of fever
- Loss of appetite
- General lethargy

triggers & irritants

- Cold, damp weather conditions, especially fog
- Air pollution
- Cigarette smoke
- Coughs and colds, or as a secondary infection after measles, chickenpox or whooping cough.
- Previous respiratory tract infections

conventional treatment

Visit your doctor, who will examine your child and listen to her chest. He may prescribe antibiotics if the bronchitis is caused by bacteria and perhaps an inhaler to help with breathing. If your child's symptoms are mild, you can take care of her yourself at home. If she has a temperature above 38°C (100.4°F) and is over 3 months old, you can give her children's paracetamol.

complementary treatments

aromatherapy

Aromatherapy oils inhaled or applied to the chest can help to control and ease the symptoms of bronchitis. The following essential oils are helpful: eucalyptus, myrtle, ravensara, niaouli and thyme linalol.

Mix together 5 drops each of thyme linalol, eucalyptus and niaouli, and 12 drops of myrtle essential oils. Put 10 drops into a bowl of hot water and put in a safe place in your child's room. Alternatively, put 2 drops on a tissue and tuck it under her pillow. You can also dilute a couple of drops in a teaspoonful of vegetable oil and massage it gently into your child's chest to help her breathing.

homeopathy

If your child has not fully recovered from a particularly debilitating attack of bronchitis, consider consulting a homeopath for advice.

Bryonia is indicated for dry coughs where there are also stabbing pains in the chest.

Phosphorous is used for dry ticklish coughs, where the child is wheezy.

Ipecac is a good remedy for babies with rattling chests and a lot of mucus which can lead to vomiting.

Ant tart is used for a rattling chest, where the phlegm is not easily shifted by coughing, and breathing is wheezy.

Pulsatilla is the best remedy where there is a lot of phlegm on the chest.

iridology

This is particularly effective for respiratory disorders. Children of the lymphatic type (see page 16) have an inherent tendency to catarrh, coughs, bronchitis and sinusitis.

herbalism

A tincture of echinacea, formulated especially for children, will boost your child's immune system. Plant infusions will ease chesty symptoms. However, any herbal treatment should be regarded as complementary and you should always seek the advice of a qualified herbalist.

common sense

• Encourage your child to rest as much as possible while she is feeling poorly.

• Using a couple of pillows, prop up your child at night so that she can breathe more easily.

• Make sure that your child is drinking enough. Offer soothing drinks, such as hot lemon and honey (only if she is over 12 months old) regularly to make sure she does not become dehydrated.

• Do not give her any cough medicines that could suppress her cough and keep phlegm in the airways.

• Keep her warm.

• Put a damp towel on the radiator in her room. A moist, steamy atmosphere will help her breathe and keep her bronchial passages clear. Alternatively, you could use a humidifier.

• Put a vaporizer in your child's room.

• Do not be alarmed if your child vomits after a fit of coughing.

• Do not expose your child to cigarette smoke or smoky places.

• If your child is not getting better, consult your doctor.

• If your child coughs up blood, her breathing becomes laboured and particularly difficult, or there is any sign of blueness around her lips, seek medical advice immediately.

colds

Colds are caused by a variety of different viruses and are probably the most common childhood ailment. The virus irritates the mucus membranes in the nose and upper respiratory tract, causing them to swell and produce even more mucus. Colds affect children of all ages at one time or another, but are a particular problem for breastfeeding babies, who find it hard to feed if their nose is blocked up. Many children suffer recurrent colds during the winter months, which can be wearing for both child and parents.

common symptoms

- Running or blocked nose
- Breathing difficulties
- Sneezing
- Tickly cough from mucus running down throat
- Sore throat and swollen glands
- Running watery eyes
- Congestion and popping in the ears
- Slight fever
- Aches and pains
- Loss of appetite
- Tiredness and irritability

triggers & irritants

- Over-tiredness and being run down (perhaps at the end of the school term)
- Tendency to catarrh
- Too many dairy products or too much sugar (particularly in younger children whose immune systems are under-developed)
- Stress
- Lack of fresh air
- Lack of exercise
- Smoky atmosphere (children of smokers have more colds)

conventional treatment

If your child has a mild cold that is not particularly bothering him, it is easy to care for him at home. However, you should contact your doctor if his symptoms do not resolve or if his temperature goes above 38°C (104°F), his ears become painful or he develops a nasty cough – these are all signs that complications are developing. It is also worth remembering that antibiotics cannot be used to treat colds.

complementary treatments

aromatherapy

• If your child is over 3 years old he can inhale essential oils.

Add 2–5 drops of essential oil (see below) to a bowl of hot water and get your child to inhale this, with a towel over his head, several times a day. Supervise your child at all times.

• The following essential oils are antiseptic and help to relieve cold symptoms: tea tree, chamomile, eucalyptus, lavender, clove, lemon, pine and thyme. Use them singly or in combination.

Add a couple of drops of eucalyptus, lemon or lavender essential oil to 1 teaspoonful of carrier oil and rub the mixture on to your child's chest.

homeopathy

Aconite is prescribed for a cold that comes on suddenly after exposure to extreme weather and where your child develops a sore throat and sneezing.

Arsenicum is used for colds where the nose runs constantly, and the nose and lips become red and sore.

Pulsatilla is the remedy for colds where the mucus is thick and yellowy green.

Nux vomica is prescribed for colds where the nose is blocked at night.

Gelsenium is used for spring colds with a heavy head and aching muscles.

Hepar sulph is for thick heavy colds with lots of yellow mucus.

western herbalism

• Turmeric helps cold symptoms, particularly sore throats.

Mix ¼ teaspoon of turmeric into some honey and let your child lick it off a spoon. Alternatively, add to herbal tea.

• Peppermint is a decongestant and will help relieve catarrh. Give your child peppermint tea.

nutritional therapy

Eating the right foods at the right time aids the healing process. This means giving your child as little food as possible at the beginning of a cold, so that his energy is directed into getting better rather than into digestive processes. This is seldom a problem because most children go off their food when they have a cold.

• If your child is hungry, give him home-made vegetable soups, fruit and fruit juices.

• Add garlic, onions and leeks to home-made soup to boost your child's immune system.

• Reduce his intake of dairy foods, especially if he has a tendency to catarrh, as they can increase mucus production.

• Leave a chopped onion in a couple of dessertspoonsful of honey for 30 minutes until softened. Drain off the liquid and give a teaspoonful to your child regularly throughout the day.

• Hot honey and lemon drinks will soothe sore throats and help to clear catarrh.

• As a preventive measure, make sure that your child's diet is rich in vitamin C by including plenty of fresh fruit.

common sense

• Keep your child warm but also try to keep your house well ventilated because fresh air is important. Make sure he is well wrapped-up and let him play outside on fine days.

• Offer your child plenty of fluids so he does not become dehydrated. Honey and lemon drinks are particularly soothing for colds.

• Work with his body – do not try to suppress symptoms but help the body in its effort to cleanse itself of the virus.

• Dab petroleum jelly around his nose to form a barrier and stop the skin becoming red and sore.

• A warm, steamy atmosphere helps, so keep up a steady routine of baths and warm drinks.

influenza

This acute infection of the airways is caused by a virus. There are a number of different strains of the flu virus but the symptoms are all very similar. Influenza can be a very debilitating illness – your child will be too exhausted to move and will complain of aches and pains. It can last for up to 2 weeks, and your child will also need plenty of time to recover.

common symptoms

- **Fever, shown by a high temperature, flushes, sweating and chills**
- **Sore, irritated eyes**
- **Headache**
- **Muscle aches and pains**
- **Intense fatigue and weakness**
- **Sore throat, cough and cold**
- **Loss of appetite**
- **Vomiting and diarrhoea (in young children)**

conventional treatments

You can treat your child at home unless she becomes really ill, in which case you should contact your doctor. A bad cough, with a lot of phlegm, indicates a secondary infection, and your doctor will usually prescribe antibiotics if it is affecting her chest.

Consult your doctor if your child develops laboured breathing, ear ache, drowsiness or a rash – or if she is asthmatic or diabetic. A bad attack of influenza can sometimes give rise to pneumonia.

complementary treatments

aromatherapy

Essential oils can be used to help symptoms and aid recovery. Ravensara, thyme, eucalyptus and niaouli are the best aromatherapy remedies for influenza. You can also diffuse anti-viral oils to reduce the chances of cross-infection in your home.

- Add 2 drops each of red thyme, oregano, cinnamon and clove to a diffuser and place it in your child's room before she goes to bed.

- Add a few drops of lavender oil to tepid water to sponge down your child's body, or add to a lukewarm bath.

- Lavender and chamomile oil will both help to reduce fever, especially if it is accompanied by a headache.

• Add eucalyptus, lavender and rosemary essential oils to water in a plant spray and spritz around your child's room at regular intervals to disinfect it.

homeopathy

There are several remedies that are really helpful if your child has flu.

Gelsenium is the remedy most often associated with influenza, and works particularly well if the child is lethargic and complaining of aches and pains.

Bryonia is prescribed when the child is irritable and thirsty and has a dry painful cough and splitting headache.

Arsenicum is for influenza when the child is restless, and feels chilly but is burning hot to touch.

western herbalism

• Echinacea is probably the best-known natural remedy for boosting resistance to influenza. It should be taken as soon as the first symptoms appear, then every 2–3 hours for the first few days.

• Garlic and thyme boost the immune system to help fight flu.

• Lime flower, elderflower and chamomile tea, as hot as possible, should be taken several times a day to enhance sweating.

nutritional therapy

A child with a fever should be given little or no food. Most children with flu have little inclination to eat because they do not have enough spare energy for the process of digestion.

Blackcurrant juice mixed with hot water is particularly beneficial because it contains large amounts of vitamin C, which enhances resistance to infection. You should give this to your child as soon as you think that she is coming down with a bout of influenza. Plain water with a squeeze of fresh lemon juice is another good drink. Once the fever has subsided, give your child fruit juices.

traditional chinese medicine

According to Chinese medicine, foods that build up resistance to influenza include home-made chicken soup and vitamin- and mineral-rich foods, such as turnips, swedes, parsnips, sardines, figs, raisins, almonds, pecans and pine nuts.

common sense

• Encourage your child to get plenty of rest and to stay in bed until she has fully recovered.

• Avoid dairy products, which increase mucus production.

• Do not worry if she does not want to eat. When her appetite returns, offer light nourishing foods, such as soup and fish.

• Offer her plenty of fruit juice and water to keep up his fluid intake.

• Keep her away from other people.

• Give her lots of tender loving care.

coughs

A child's cough is usually nothing to worry about – it is either a simple clearing of the throat or a symptom of a passing respiratory infection. There are two types of cough: a dry cough, which produces nothing; and a productive cough, which produces phlegm. However, a persistent night-time cough can indicate a more serious problem, such as asthma, so it is always important to get it checked out. Watch your child carefully and note any particular characteristics of the cough, as well as any general changes.

common symptoms

- A dry, irritating, non-productive cough that may become looser and rattly
- Worsening of the cough at night
- Vomiting as a result of coughing attacks that bring up phlegm
- Wheezing, breathing difficulties or high temperature
- White or yellow phlegm
- Loss of appetite
- General lethargy

triggers & irritants

- Colds and respiratory tract infections
- Immunizations for whooping cough and polio
- Cold, damp weather, especially fog
- Air pollution
- Cigarette smoke

conventional treatment

Over-the-counter cough medicines can help to loosen phlegm but avoid any that are suppressive. If your child is less than a year old, or if you are worried about his cough – particularly if he shows signs of wheezing or other breathing difficulties – consult your doctor. She will check out your child for the following: a chest infection if the cough has turned chesty and breathing is laboured; asthma if he wheezes and coughs persistently at night; croup if the cough is a sudden barking one that comes on at night; whooping cough if he has coughing spasms, particularly at night, that result in vomiting.

complementary treatments

aromatherapy

Essential oils can be used in your child's bath, for steam inhalations and in vaporizers. Choose from chamomile, eucalyptus, lavender, pine and thyme.

Mix together 10 drops each of ravensara and eucalyptus radiata and 5 drops of niaouli with 1 tablespoonful of vegetable oil. Use 4–8 drops as a chest and back rub (4 drops for under 2s, 6 drops for 3–7 year-olds, then 8 drops). Add 8 drops to a bowl of steaming hot water and leave in your child's room overnight, well out of her reach. Try putting 1 drop on a tissue and tucking it under her pillow at night.

homeopathy

There are many remedies for coughs. Here are some of the common ones.

For dry coughs:

Aconite for dry, barking coughs that come on during the night.

Spongia for dry suffocating coughs.

Bryonia for dry, hacking coughs that are painful and worse when lying down.

Phosphorous for dry, tickly coughs triggered by changes of temperature

For wet loose coughs:

Pulsatilla for coughs that produce a lot of yellow-green coloured phlegm.

Ipecac for spasmodic coughs where the chest is rattly and there is a lot of mucus.

Ant tart where there is a lot of phlegm on the chest and non-productive coughing.

herbalism

The herbal treatment of coughs works by speeding up the body's own healing processes and helping to clear the chest of phlegm, while simultaneously boosting the immune system.

• Echinacea, turmeric, ginger, cinnamon, cloves, eucalyptus, hyssop and thyme will all help your child to fight infection and inflammation in the chest. These can be taken as a tea to help reduce feverish symptoms.

• Comfrey leaf, linseed, licorice, marshmallow and wild cherry bark, taken as an infusion or a syrup, will ease dry coughs. Add relaxing herbs such as chamomile and lavender at night.

• Warming or stimulating herbs, such as cinnamon, fennel, ginger or cloves, taken as a hot tea, will help catarrhal coughs by loosening mucus.

• Echinacea will boost your child's immune system.

• Soften a chopped onion in a couple of dessertspoonsful of honey for 30 minutes. Drain off the liquid and give your child a teaspoonful at regular intervals.

nutritional therapy

If your child has a fever as well as a cough, give him plenty to drink and avoid solid foods. Once he is feeling better, give him light foods, such as vegetable soup, and plenty of fresh fruit. Avoid dairy products, which are thought to increase mucus production.

bach flower remedies

Add a few drops of Rescue Remedy to a glass of water and give to your child whenever necessary.

common sense

• Encourage your child to blow his nose regularly to prevent mucus draining down his throat.

• Give him an extra pillow to raise his head if his cough is worse at night.

• Offer plenty of soothing drinks, such as honey and lemon in hot water.

• Keep the air in his room moist by putting a damp towel on the radiator or using a vaporizer.

• If your child is having difficulty bringing up phlegm, place him over your knee and gently pat his back.

• Give him plenty to drink to avoid dehydration.

• Do not use any cough medicines that act as a suppressant, thus preventing him from bringing up phlegm.

hay fever

Hay fever (or seasonal rhinitis) is an allergic reaction to pollen. This irritates the mucus membranes of the nose, eyes and airways, releasing histamine and leading to inflammation and swelling. Although hay fever often starts during the teenage years, it is now getting more common among younger children and the number of sufferers is continuing to rise. However, it rarely occurs in children below the age of 5 years. Hay fever tends to run in families and an increase in environmental pollution is thought to be a contributory factor.

common symptoms

- Itchy nose, mouth, throat and eyes as the weather gets warmer
- Frequent sneezing, blocked nose, stuffiness and congestion
- Runny nose with clear mucus
- Breathing difficulties – wheezing or worsening of an existing condition such as asthma
- Red, sore, gritty eyes, often bloodshot and watery as well as itchy
- Stuffiness in the head
- General feeling of being under the weather

Warning If your child's breathing becomes difficult or there is any swelling of the lips or throat, seek immediate medical attention.

triggers & irritants

- Pollen (of trees and grasses)
- Fungal spores
- Hot dry weather (when the pollen count rises)
- Family history of hay fever, asthma, eczema and psoriasis
- Tendency to catarrh or frequent upper respiratory tract infections
- Poor nutrition
- Sugar
- Wheat and dairy products
- Allergies to certain foods or household products

conventional treatment

Your doctor can prescribe treatments such as eye drops and nasal sprays containing steroids, and antihistamine tablets. However, these may supress symptoms, which may worsen once the medication has worn off. She can also arrange allergy tests to identify the exact trigger of your child's attacks.

complementary treatments

nutritional therapy

Boost your child's immune system by making sure that he has a healthy, balanced diet. Some experts believe that the rise in hay fever is linked to increased consumption of sugar. Eliminating wheat from the diet during the hay-fever season may also help to reduce symptoms.

aromatherapy

Essential oils can help to relieve irritation and allow your child to sleep at night. Experiment to find what best suits him. The following oils can help: lemon, lavender, geranium, neroli, Roman chamomile, tangerine, eucalyptus, mandarin, rosemary and grapefruit.

Mix together 4 drops of Roman chamomile, 4 drops of lemon and 2 drops of lavender essential oils. Put a couple of drops on to a tissue for your child to sniff throughout the day. You can also add this mixture to his bathwater to relieve congestion.

homeopathy

It is advisable to consult a qualified homeopath if you are unsure. She will usually recommend treating hay fever during the winter months, in order to lessen the severity of the symptoms in spring and summer. A number of years of this approach is thought to cure the condition, eliminating the symptoms altogether.

Many people use over-the-counter 'hay-fever mixture' preparations available in health-food stores. The following remedies may also help:

Nux vomica is used when the nose runs during the day and is blocked up at night, when there is frequent sneezing, and internal itching of the nose and ears.

Pulsatilla is for a thick discharge from the nose, particularly when the child is outside. He also feels miserable and under the weather.

Allium cepa is prescribed when the nose has a burning discharge and the eyes have a watery discharge.

Arsenicum is used where the discharge from the nose has made the lips and nostrils very red and sore.

Euphrasia is used when the eyes are so watery they become red and sore.

western herbalism

• Chamomile is one of the herbs that can boost the immune system and help to build resistance to allergies. It needs to be taken over several months for the best results.

Add a chamomile teabag to a cup of boiling water and infuse for 10 minutes. Give your child 3 cups of this every day, before meals.

• Nettles also have a good reputation for calming allergenic responses. They can be used in teas, soups and stews, or taken in capsule form.

naturopathy

• Vitamin C and magnesium are natural antihistamines. Foods rich in these can help with allergic symptoms.

• Try desensitizing your child before the start of the hay fever season. Honey contains pollen, so try giving your child a dessertspoonful of honey with each meal in the 2–4 months leading up to the hay fever season. Locally produced honey is best since it contains the types of pollens to which your child will be most exposed. Continue this throughout the season.

kinesiology

This holistic technique is effective in identifying allergies. The practitioner will explain the benefits of nutritional supplements, homeopathic remedies and flower essences.

bach flower remedies

Crab Apple helps where there are feelings of being contaminated.

common sense

• Check your child's temperature: a raised temperature probably indicates a cold or other infection.

• Place a facecloth wrung out in cold water over your child's eyes to soothe the itching sensation.

• Smear petroleum jelly around your child's nose and on his lips to help with the soreness.

• Keep a gel-filled eye mask in the fridge.

• Vacuum your home regularly to keep it pollen free.

• Limit your child's exposure to allergens by keeping windows closed at night when possible.

• Watch the pollen count reports. When pollen counts are high, avoid grassy and leafy areas and newly mown lawns. Do not let your child play outside at peak times – usually first thing in the morning and mid to late afternoon.

allergic rhinitis

Rhinitis is an inflammation of the mucus membrane lining the nose. It can be either seasonal (see hay fever, page 96) or perennial, meaning that your child is affected all year round. More and more cases of allergic rhinitis are being reported – experts believe this is due to environmental and lifestyle issues.

common symptoms

- Constantly running itchy nose, with clear mucus
- Blocked nose
- Sneezing, particularly on waking
- Breathing through the mouth
- Stuffy head

triggers & irritants

- Pet fur, dander and saliva
- House dust mite
- Mould, in damp conditions
- Certain foods
- Household products
- Tendency to catarrh or frequent respiratory infections
- Weak digestion, poor nutrition or poor general health (rhinitis is related to the immune system)
- Genetics - if both parents have allergies, your child's odds of developing them are 75%

conventional treatment

If you suspect your child is showing symptoms of allergic rhinitis, your doctor can prescribe eye drops and nasal sprays, which contain steroids, and antihistamine tablets. He can also arrange allergy testing.

complementary treatments

homeopathy

Nux vomica is recommended when the nose runs during the day and is blocked at night, and where there is frequent sneezing and itchy nose and ears.

Pulsatilla will help when there is a thick discharge from the nose, particularly when the child is outdoors, and when he feels stuffed up indoors. The child will also feel miserable and under the weather.

herbalism

- Herbs such as chamomile can boost the immune system and help to build resistance to allergies.

Add a chamomile teabag to a cup of boiling water and infuse for 10 minutes. Your child should drink a cup before every meal.

- Nettles also have a good reputation for calming allergic responses. They can be used in teas, soups and stews or taken in capsule form.

naturopathy

Vitamin C (found in fruit) and magnesium (found in green leafy vegetables, nuts and seeds) are natural antihistamines and can help with allergic symptoms.

kinesiology

A kinesiologist can identify allergens, pinpoint the problem and make dietary and other recommendations.

diabetes

Diabetes is on the increase, especially in children. If you are diabetic you have difficulty regulating your blood sugar levels because of a deficency or a lack of the hormone insulin. As a result, you have an abnormally high level of the sugar glucose in your blood. This can lead to a variety of problems, including impaired circulation. Almost all affected children have Type 1 (insulin-dependent) diabetes.

common symptoms

- **Frequent urination**
- **Excessive thirst**
- **Tiredness**
- **Weight loss**
- **Smell of acetone (nail-varnish remover) on the breath**

triggers & irritants

- **Deficiency or total lack of insulin**
- **Excess weight**
- **Family history of diabetes – current opinion is that one in four children is genetically susceptible**
- **It's thought there is a link with milk consumption – the highest incidence of diabetes is found in Finland, which also has the world's highest consumption of milk products**

conventional treatment

Diabetes must be treated with great care. Your doctor will check the level of glucose in your child's blood. If it is too high, she may need insulin injections every day to bring it under control. She will probably also be given a device for measuring her blood sugar levels.

complementary treatments

The suitability of any complementary treatments depends on the individual child and the medication required. In the best scenario, the symptoms can sometimes be controlled through diet alone.

nutritional therapy

Vegetarians are less likely to develop diabetes, and a vegetarian diet can also be successful in treating the condition, sometimes even reversing it. Children should have a wholefood diet based on regular meals with plenty of starchy carbohydrates and fibre, and not too much fat or sugar. Supplements of vitamin E can help to reduce the effects of excess blood sugar. The mineral chromium can also help to regulate blood sugar. Always consult your doctor before giving your child any supplements.

homeopathy

A homeopath will look at the individual child and her symptoms, and suggest an appropriate remedy.

common sense

- If your child is old enough, she may be able to give herself the injections. However, you must also learn how to do this as well.

- If your child shows signs of low blood sugar (hypoglycaemia), give her sugary drinks or foods, such as honey, soft sweets or glucose tablets.

colic

Colic is a fairly common condition in new babies, affecting about one in five. The baby becomes very uncomfortable and will cry continually. It is characterized by a griping pain in the abdomen, which is thought to be caused by trapped wind, and affects both breastfed and bottle-fed babies. It occurs mostly in the first 12 weeks but, in some cases, can carry on for months.

common symptoms

- Legs thrashing or drawn up to the stomach, clenched fists
- Baby out of sorts, particularly after 6pm
- Flushed red face
- Intense crying that can go on for hours
- Hard abdomen
- Baby wants to feed constantly
- Discomfort after feeding
- Poor sleeping patterns

triggers & irritants

- Traumatic birth
- Premature birth
- Gulping milk and taking in a lot of air
- Reaction to a food substance in your breast milk
- Trapped wind

conventional treatment

This includes winding your baby over your shoulder, walking around with him, and giving him a dummy or colic drops. Always contact your doctor if your baby is unwell in other ways, for example if he is vomiting or suffering from diarrhoea.

complementary treatments

aromatherapy

A warm bath with diluted essential oils will help to relax and comfort your baby.

Mix 1 drop of cardamom and 1 drop of lavender essential oils into a teaspoonful of carrier oil, and add a ¼ teaspoonful to his bath. Swish over his stomach.

homeopathy

Chamomilla is indicated for a baby who is very upset by the pains and is soothed only by being carried around.

Stramonium is helpful if he had a traumatic birth and seems angry.

osteopathy

The baby's cranium can be compressed during birth, which can give rise to the symptoms of colic. Consider taking your baby to see a cranial osteopath. This gentle style of manipulation is often very successful in calming colic.

chiropractic

Babies respond very well to gentle work on the spine. Chiropractic can help any kind of pain relating to the skeletal and nervous systems, and brings great relief to indigestion.

bach flower remedies

Apply Rescue Remedy to your baby's temples, wrists and stomach to help soothe and relax him.

western herbalism

Try giving your baby a herbal tea before feeds to help his digestion and again after the feed if he still seems unhappy. If you drink a slightly stronger version of this tea yourself, it will pass through your breast milk to your baby. Choose from chamomile, fennel or lemon balm tea.

Use a ¼ teaspoonful of herbs to 100 ml (about 3 fl. oz) boiling water and allow to cool. Strain and give in a bottle.

nutritional therapy

Your baby may be reacting to a substance in your breast milk. Breastfeeding mothers should consider cutting out the following items from their diet, because all are known to have a detrimental effect on babies: citrus fruit, spicy foods, brassicas (such as cabbage and cauliflower), onions, garlic, chocolate and caffeinated drinks. Make sure you eat regularly, with healthy snacks between meals. Drink plenty of water.

Alternatively, your baby could be reacting to the cow's milk in formula feed, in which case you may have to find an alternative.

reflexology

Reflexology can help a baby to release any tension after a traumatic birth and to adjust to life outside the womb. Babies respond well to reflexology as they are highly receptive to touch. Daily sessions can boost your baby's sense of well-being and help with the stress of colic.

massage

This can be used as both a curative and a preventive measure. It will relax your baby's abdomen and relieve colic, wind and other symptoms of abdominal tension. Lay your baby face-down in the crook of your arm while gently kneading his abdomen with your other hand to help with the discomfort. You can also walk around with your baby in this position, which will bring him further relief.

common sense

• Play some favourite music to help soothe your baby.

• Lay your baby stomach-down across your knees on a well-wrapped hot water bottle.

constipation

There is no fixed rule about the number of times your child has a bowel movement because no two children are the same. Most have a bowel movement at least once a day. Others seem more prone to have a bowel movement only every few days, and this can affect them from a very early age. Children are usually described as constipated if they have very irregular bowel movements and difficulty in passing a stool, and if the stool is hard and dry, with a pebble-like texture.

common symptoms

- Unusually long interval between bowel movements
- Hard stools that are difficult to pass
- Abdominal discomfort and stomach ache, often at mealtimes
- Bad breath
- Muscle aches
- Lethargy
- Irritability

triggers & irritants

- Lack of fibre or too much refined food
- Food intolerance, particularly to wheat
- Dehydration from not drinking enough water
- Vitamin C and magnesium deficiency
- Change of diet
- Moving on to solids
- Potty-training
- Ignoring the urge to visit the toilet
- Anxiety about going to the toilet
- Travelling or change of routine
- Lack of exercise
- Emotional stress

conventional treatment

Consult your doctor if this in an on-going problem. He may prescribe laxatives or senna for your child.

complementary treatments

nutritional therapy

• Encourage your child to eat more fibre. Introduce more fresh fruit and vegetables, and wholegrains such as brown rice and oats into her diet. If your child does not like brown rice, mix it with white rice until she gets used to it. Give her snacks of dried fruit, such as raisins and apricots. Prunes are a tried and tested remedy – if necessary, disguise them in a banana and prune smoothie.

• Give your child live yogurt to help balance intestinal bacteria.

• Dehydration is one of the commonest causes of constipation. If you think that your child is not drinking enough, give her a beaker of water or diluted fruit juice and keep reminding her to take sips so you can monitor her fluid intake.

homeopathy

Bryonia is helpful where the stools are hard and dry.

Nux vomica is the remedy when a child has the urge to pass a stool but fails to do so.

chinese herbalism

Chinese herbalists believe that constipation is caused by a food blockage in babies and weak liver energy in older children. Constipation can also be the result of kidney disorders and emotional problems if there is some deficiency in the kidney *chi*.

reflexology

Reflexology can be a great help with constipation. The manipulative techniques relax the pressure points, helping the body to relax. This is vital for healthy, regular bowel movements.

massage

Massaging the abdomen is an ideal way to help your child's constipation, and she will also find the touch soothing. If it is not too tender, try massaging the whole of her stomach with a gentle circular movement, working around the navel. Use an essential oil mix, made by adding 1 drop petitgrain, 2 drops mandarin and 2 drops lemon to 1 teaspoonful of carrier oil. The petitgrain is anti-spasmodic, the lemon revitalizing and the mandarin emotionally comforting.

western herbalism

• For children over 12 months old, a teaspoonful of honey in a cup of hot water first thing in the morning is a pleasant remedy for mild constipation.

• Herbs that bulk out the stool, so that it is easier to pass, include psyllium seeds and flax seeds. Add 1 teaspoonful to a cup of warm water and, once the seeds have swollen, give them to your child before she goes to bed.

• Herbs such as chamomile, fennel, ginger and peppermint are relaxing and, when sipped as a tea, can bring relief to a tense bowel.

common sense

• Do not make a big fuss about your child going to the toilet.

• Do not give your child laxatives, drugs or suppositories. Instead make changes to her diet.

• Make sure that she drinks plenty of water to keep her stools soft.

diarrhoea

Diarrhoea has many causes and is quite common in young children. It tends to last about 24 hours and starts when the lining of the bowel becomes inflamed. As a result, waste passes through it too quickly, taking a lot of liquid with it. There are two types of diarrhoea: the acute form, which is caused by anxiety, food poisoning and medicines; and the chronic form, which is usually a sign of an intestinal disorder.

common symptoms

- Unpleasant-smelling, loose stools or liquid faeces
- Frequent bowel movements
- Stomach cramps
- Bloating and flatulence

triggers & irritants

- Over-eating the wrong foods
- Food intolerance
- Excessive fruit or fruit juice
- Food-poisoning
- Bacterial or viral stomach infection such as gastroenteritis
- Colds and coughs
- Nervousness and anxiety
- Teething
- Antibiotics

conventional treatment

Medication to control symptoms and rehydration sachets to restore fluid balance are available over the counter. However, you should seek medical advice if your child continually passes loose stools or has prolonged diarrhoea because this is not normal.

Warning If your child vomits and there is blood in the stools, call a doctor immediately.

complementary treatments

homeopathy

Aloes is indicated for a child who feels anxious and has a lot of wind with the diarrhoea.

Arsenicum is helpful when the diarrhoea is triggered by food-poisoning or eating too much fruit.

Podophylum is the remedy when the diarrhoea is explosive, green and watery.

Chamomilla is helpful for diarrhoea in teething babies.

nutritional therapy

Do not worry if your child does not want to eat, as he will get his appetite back eventually. Offer him plain water and rehydration drinks to replace the lost fluids and minerals – perhaps adding a little fruit juice to improve the taste. Once the bowel has settled down, give your child easily digestible meals, such as yogurt, white rice and toast. Avoid milk, apart from breast milk, and rich, fatty foods. If you think that a food intolerance is causing the diarrhoea, consult a qualified nutritionist, who will help to identify the problem.

western herbalism

• Echinacea can help your child's immune system to ward off infection.

Make a cleansing drink by adding a ¼ teaspoonful of grated ginger, half a lemon and 1 teaspoonful of honey to a cup of boiled water.

• Make a soothing yogurt drink with half a cupful of live yogurt, half a cupful of water, a teaspoonful of freshly grated nutmeg, and a pinch each of cinnamon and ginger.

traditional chinese medicine

The practitioner will prescribe herbs to strengthen any weakness in the stomach and spleen. Diarrhoea may suggest spleen, kidney or liver disharmonies.

kinesiology

If the diarrhoea is caused by a food intolerance, a kinesiologist can help to pinpoint allergens and prescribe a nutritional plan.

reflexology

Some simple hand exercises that work on the relevant reflexes for digestion can help to relieve the pain and tension associated with diarrhoea.

aromatherapy

• Try this soothing tummy rub if your child is stressed.

Dilute 1 drop of Roman chamomile, 2 drops of eucalyptus and 3 drops of lavender essential oils in 1 tablespoon vegetable oil. Use a small amount to rub over your child's abdomen.

common sense

Check for symptoms of dehydration, such as a fever.

stomach ache

This common childhood complaint is caused by either physical or emotional factors. In most cases, it disappears of its own accord. Children under the age of 2 years are less likely to complain of stomach ache, but even older children tend to be rather vague about the exact nature of the pain.

common symptoms

- Crying and drawing up the legs
- Pale skin
- Vomiting
- Headache
- Sleepiness

triggers & irritants

- Indigestion caused by eating too quickly
- Over-eating, especially the wrong types of foods
- Too much seasonal fruit, such as plums or strawberries
- Food-poisoning
- Drinking cold water
- Over-excitement, upset and stress

conventional treatment

Consult your doctor if you are worried about your child's stomach ache or it keeps recurring. This is particularly important if the pain is severe, it hurts when you press on your child's abdomen, she is continually vomiting or she is under 2 years old.

complementary treatments

traditional chinese medicine

According to Chinese medicine, the stomach is responsible for rotting and ripening food. If the stomach *chi* 'rebels', the food will move upwards, leading to problems such as hiccups, nausea and vomiting. Cold food puts a strain on the stomach, and insufficiently chewed or indigestible food will also cause problems.

iridology

This is particularly effective for treating digestive disorders. Children who are of the biliary type (see page 17) have an inherent tendency to flatulence, constipation, colitis and other gastro-intestinal weaknesses. The iridologist will help your child to learn about her weaknesses and become more aware of what she can do to help herself. The iridologist will advise on the best ways of reversing existing conditions and managing inherent weaknesses.

western herbalism

Soothing herbal teas, such as chamomile, lemon balm and peppermint, are an excellent remedy for settling the stomach and calming the child.

bach flower remedies

If the cause of the stomach ache is emotional, Rescue Remedy can relieve anxiety encourage the body to heal itself.

threadworms

This common parasitic infection tends to affect children between the ages of 5 and 10 years. The tiny, thread-like worms resemble pieces of white cotton and are often found around the anus, although they can live in any part of the digestive tract. The eggs are easily passed on to other people, so finger nails should be kept short and scrubbed every day with a nail brush.

common symptoms

- Itching of the anus, especially at night
- Sore red anus
- Scratching around the bottom
- Thin, white threads in the stools – often moving
- Abdominal pain, mild colicky pain
- Bad breath
- Irritability
- Disturbed sleep
- Weight loss and increased appetite

triggers & irritants

- Contact with contaminated objects, such as toilet seats

conventional treatment

Your doctor will prescribe medication for the whole family, or you can buy over-the-counter remedies from a pharmacy.

complementary treatments

aromatherapy

A bath is a great soother for a sore anus.

Add 8 drops of cardamom and 6 drops of Roman chamomile essential oils to 2 teaspoonsful of vegetable oil. Add a ¼ teaspoonful to your child's bath.

homeopathy

Cina (wormseed) is the first remedy to consider.

Teucrium can be used after Cina if the worms keep reappearing.

nutritional therapy

Worms flourish on sugar, so reduce the amount of sugary foods and other refined carbohydrates in your child's diet. Encourage her to eat plenty of fresh fruit and vegetables. Give her live yogurt daily to enhance her bowel health.

western herbalism

Make a soothing lotion to relieve itching around the anus.

Add a couple of drops of eucalyptus, lavender or tea tree essential oil to some calendula cream and apply at night.

traditional chinese medicine

According to Chinese medicine, pumpkin seeds are a gentle and effective remedy for cleansing the body of worms. Try adding some to your child's breakfast cereal.

vomiting

There is nothing unusual about a child being sick and it's usually often a case of over-indulgence. It is also the body's way of ridding itself of infection or toxins. However, repeated or severe vomiting is a cause for concern, and can quickly lead to dehydration.

common symptoms

- Nausea
- Dry, parched lips
- Stomach ache
- Reduced urination
- Diarrhoea
- Fever
- Refusing to drink

triggers & irritants

- Over-eating, especially the wrong types of food
- Food-poisoning or a stomach bug
- Over-excitement
- Weak stomach

conventional treatment

Most cases of vomiting can be safely treated at home. However, if there is blood in the vomit, severe stomach pain, indications of dehydration or the vomiting is prolonged, consult your doctor.

complementary treatments

aromatherapy

Essential oils that help nausea include ginger, peppermint, spearmint, cardamom and lavender.

Add 2 drops each of lavender and cardamom essential oils to 600 ml (20 fl. oz) of lukewarm water. Wring out a cloth in this solution and use it as a compress on your child's forehead (over 2s only).

homeopathy

Arsenicum is usually the first remedy to consider for sickness and diarrhoea from food-poisoning

western herbalism

Ginger, lemon balm and peppermint teas help with the symptoms of nausea.

acupressure

A simple technique for helping with nausea is to lightly press the acupressure point on your child's wrist with your fingertips.

chiropractic

If your child is repeatedly vomiting but there is no obvious cause, a chiropractor can check his spine to see if anything else is triggering the sickness. She can then use manipulation to control the situation.

travel sickness

Also known as motion sickness, this can be triggered by any form of travel: cars, boats, planes, trains — even theme-park rides. This common problem is caused by the repetitive motion upsetting the balance mechanisms in the inner ear, leading to disorientation and dizziness. Car travel causes most problems and is usually compounded by exhaust fumes. Your child may get tense at the very thought of travelling. Encourage him to look out of the window rather than looking down to help his balance mechanism work properly.

common symptoms

- **Dizziness and faintness**
- **Nausea or actual vomiting**
- **Cold, clammy skin**
- **Ear ache**

triggers & irritants

- **Nervousness about travel**
- **Petrol and diesel fumes**
- **Hot weather**

conventional treatment

Over-the-counter remedies are available at pharmacies. Be sure to ask for one suitable for children.

complementary treatments

aromatherapy

Put 4–5 drops of ginger essential oil on a tissue pad for your child to inhale.

bach flower remedies

Rescue Remedy is a good all-rounder for stressful situations. Try Aspen (for fear of the unknown) or Rock Rose (for panic).

Add 2 drops of your chosen remedy to a small bottle filled with water. Give your child 4 drops of this mixture in a little water as and when he needs it.

western herbalism

Ginger is a wonderfully effective remedy for travel sickness.

For children over 2 years old, make a tea using one peppermint teabag and one ginger teabag. Leave to stand for 5–10 minutes, then cool and put it into a drinking cup suitable for the journey.

acupressure

Wristbands can help with nausea — especially seasickness — as they work on the Chinese principle of acupressure. The bands press on specific pressure points on the wrist. Alternatively, you can massage the *neiguan* point. This is positioned three finger-widths above the upper wrist crease on the inside of the arm, between the two tendons.

food allergy

A food allergy is a hypersensitive reaction to a particular food. The number of people with food allergies is on the increase – in the UK alone it is estimated to affect about 2 per cent of children. Unfortunately, children often develop a reaction to the food they most enjoy, so make a note if your child has any particular favourites. The reaction is usually immediate. Eating or drinking the problem food triggers an immune response that produces symptoms affecting the skin, respiratory system, cardiovascular system and gastro-intestinal tract.

common symptoms

- Itchy rash, eczema or urticaria
- Swelling, particularly eyelids and lips
- Stomach ache
- Vomiting and diarrhoea
- Runny nose and chronic catarrh
- Wheezing
- Insomnia
- Temper tantrums, behavioural problems, hyperactivity and attention deficit and hyperactivity disorder
- Anaphylactic shock

Warning Anaphylactic shock is an extreme reaction that can occur within seconds of a child swallowing an allergen. Symptoms include swelling of the mouth, throat and upper body. This is a life-threatening condition requiring immediate medical help. Susceptible people are usually advised to carry adrenaline or antihistamine tablets in case of further attacks.

triggers & irritants

- Exposure to allergens at a young age
- Cow's milk, eggs (often short term)
- Peanuts (usually permanent)
- Wheat (gluten)
- Seafood
- Strawberries and kiwi fruit
- Tomatoes
- Chocolate
- Soya
- Food colourings, flavourings, additives and preservatives, especially tartrazine and benzoate
- Artificial sweeteners
- Allergy in another family member

conventional treatment

If you suspect that your child has an allergy, seek medical advice to determine the cause. Your doctor may refer your child for skin-prick tests or blood tests. He will usually prescribe antihistamines to deal with the immediate symptoms.

complementary treatments

acupuncture

This can be effective when the underlying cause is a disharmony that is disturbing your child's *chi*. It can help to boost her immune system and restore energy levels.

nutritional therapy

Many common childhood ailments are caused by food allergies and these can be pinpointed by a nutritionist. Illness can be avoided simply by eliminating the problem substance from your child's diet. If the therapist finds a number of allergens, your child could be suffering from toxic overload. A healthy, balanced diet will give her immune system a boost. Remember to avoid all problem foods and to check labels meticulously.

Children often suffer from deficiencies of the following: vitamins A, B and C, calcium, magnesium, manganese and zinc. If you feel that your child isn't eating enough of the right foods, consider supplementing her diet with a multi-vitamin preparation.

naturopathy

Naturopathy recognises the importance of correcting the underlying disturbance of immunity. Reduction to exposure of allergens is suggested to bring immediate relief. Nutritional advice to improve the functioning of the immune system is usually offered, together with herbal and homeopathic remedies.

iridology

Haematogenic types (see page 17) have an inherent tendency to be intolerant to cow's milk. Iridology can help children to learn about their weaknesses and become more aware of how they can help themselves. The iridologist will advise on the best ways of reversing existing conditions and dealing with inherent weaknesses.

kinesiology

Health kinesiology can help identify allergies by means of a series of tests. The therapist will check your child for nutritional deficiencies and advise you about elimination diets and nutritional supplements.

common sense

- Breastfeed your baby for as long as possible.

- When pregnant and breastfeeding, avoid foods that are common allergens, such as nuts.

- Do not introduce any of the common allergens into your baby's diet until she is 6 months old.

- Keep her away from known allergens.

- Try giving her a ½ teaspoonful of bicarbonate of soda in a small glass of water up to three times every 2 hours.

food intolerance

Food intolerance – an adverse reaction to a specific food – is on the increase, for reasons that are not entirely understood. Experts think that food sensitivity is a reaction to a number of things, including poor nutrition and environmental issues such as pollution. Interestingly, it is often the most common foods that are the problem, usually because they are eaten several times a day. As a result, the body becomes over-loaded and develops a resistance to a particular food as a self-protection measure.

common symptoms

- Abdominal pain
- Wind or bloating
- Diarrhoea or constipation
- Eczema
- Hives or skin rashes around the mouth
- Wheezing
- Headaches
- Mood swings, depression and anxiety
- Lethargy and fatigue
- Cravings

triggers & irritants

- Wheat (gluten)
- Dairy foods (lactose)
- Junk and processed foods
- Sugar
- Additives, flavourings and preservatives
- Digestive enzyme deficiencies (this is quite rare)
- Stress
- Antibiotics
- Exposure to pesticides
- Exposure to pollution

conventional treatment

Most children who are food-sensitive have problems with about one to five foods. Reactions tend to be milder than in the case of food allergy. If you suspect that your child has a food sensitivity, keep a food diary for a couple of weeks to try to pinpoint the problem. Then ask your doctor to refer your child to hospital for tests. Elimination diets are not suitable for children under 5 years old, so always consult a nutritionist before embarking on any programme. Likewise, if you are thinking about cutting out a key food, such as milk, always consult a specialist first.

complementary treatments

nutritional therapy

Once you have identified the problem, review your child's diet to check it is healthy and balanced. Give him complex carbohydrates, such as porridge, brown rice, sweet potato and wholemeal spaghetti, which will raise his blood sugar slowly. Make sure he is getting plenty of good-quality protein, such as chicken, fish and lentils, to satisfy his appetite. A regular daily intake of fresh fruit and vegetables (raw wherever possible) completes the nutritional picture. Encourage your child to chew properly, avoid big meals, and anticipate his cravings by offering a healthy low-carbohydrate snack.

bach flower remedies

Try Crab Apple (for cleansing and detoxification of the body), Rock Water (for self-denial) or Olive (for mental and physical exhaustion).

western herbalism

Peppermint reduces the symptoms of bloating and wind, and also relaxes muscle tension in the colon, which helps to relieve spasms.

To boost your child's digestion, infuse a dessertspoonful of dried peppermint leaves in 150 ml (5 fl. oz) boiling water, leave to brew for 15 minutes, strain and give him a cupful after every meal.

kinesiology

Health kinesiology can help to resolve digestive problems, identify allergies and look at the individual's nutritional needs. Therapists can detect imbalances that are too subtle to show up in medical tests and will give advice on nutritional supplements.

bed-wetting

There is usually no medical reason for bed-wetting, which is more common among boys. It happens to children over the age of 3 or 4 years who have already developed bladder control, and it is frequently related to stress or a change of circumstances.

triggers & irritants

- **Stress – new baby, starting school, family arguments**
- **Urinary tract infection**
- **Immature bladder function – if your child has never been regularly dry at night**
- **Dietary deficiencies, particularly calcium and magnesium**
- **Food allergy**
- **Diabetes**
- **Getting cold at night – make sure your child is always well covered**

conventional treatment

Consult your doctor if you think your child has an infection. If the problem continues, he may refer your child for investigations. Once your child is older, usually over 7 years, the doctor may try the psychological approach of cognitive bladder training.

complementary treatments

homeopathy

Kreosotum is indicated for children who sleep deeply and are unable to wake when they need to urinate.

Equisetum is helpful where there are few distinguishing features and the child dreams about urinating while wetting the bed.

bach flower remedies

Flower remedies may be helpful by focusing on the emotional causes that could be behind bed-wetting. Try Mimulus (for fear of darkness and being alone), Aspen (for fear of the unknown and nightmares), Star of Bethlehem (for distress and unhappiness) or Sweet Chestnut (for anguish).

western herbalism

Californian poppy preparations are recommended for the treatment of repeated bed-wetting, but it is advisable to consult a medical herbalist before giving this plant to your child.

Add 1 teaspoonful of the dried plant to a cup of boiling water. Leave to infuse for 10 minutes, then strain, and offer to your child before bedtime.

If you feel the bed-wetting stems from an emotional disturbance, try lemon balm before bedtime to calm and relax him, and help to soothe his nerves.

chiropractic

If there is no obvious cause for your child's bed-wetting, consult a chiropractor in case she has any spinal or pelvic bone misalignment. The therapist may recommend X-rays and blood and urine tests to help with the diagnosis. Treatment consists of physically manipulating the bones.

osteopathy

Osteopaths have great success in dealing with bed-wetting. They treat children by manipulating misaligned bones and joints in order to bring the body back into balance.

common sense

• Do not let your child have too much to drink at bedtime.

• Star charts are a good incentive for rewarding dry nights.

• Give your child plenty of love and reassurance, as it can be very humiliating for him to wake up and discover that he has wet the bed.

urinary tract infections

Urinary tract infections are generally caused by *E. coli* bacteria from the bowel getting into the urinary system, but they can also be triggered by a viral or fungal infection. They can affect the kidneys, bladder, ureter and urethra. Cystitis (in girls) and urethritis (in boys) are the most common types of urinary tract infection.

common symptoms

- Burning or stinging sensation on urinating
- Strong-smelling sometimes cloudy urine
- Frequent urge to urinate
- Bladder does not feel fully empty after urinating
- Bed-wetting
- Blood in the urine (occasionally)
- Lower back pain
- Stomach ache and nausea
- Headache and general malaise

triggers & irritants

- Viral or fungal infection
- Not drinking enough
- Food allergy
- Thrush
- Diarrhoea
- Antibiotics

conventional treatment

At the first sign of a urinary tract infection, take your child to the doctor for a urine test. This involves dipping a diagnostic strip into a urine sample to detect the presence of an infection. Always tell the doctor: if your child finds it painful passing water; if he is experiencing increasing pains in the abdomen or lower back; if he is developing a fever or feels generally unwell; and if there is blood in his urine. These symptoms could indicate a kidney infection, in which case the doctor may issue your child with antibiotics or refer him to hospital for further investigations.

complementary treatments

aromatherapy

Tea tree oil has strong anti-bacterial and anti-fungal properties. Add it to your child's bath to help soothe the symptoms of the infection.

Add 3 drops of tea tree essential oil to 1 teaspoonful of vegetable oil and swirl the mixture into his bathwater.

homeopathy

Cantharis is the best-known remedy for urinary tract infections.

Pulsatilla is indicated for mild cystitis where there is some discomfort.

nutritional therapy

• Cranberry juice is packed with vitamin C, a powerful anti-oxidant that helps to keep the immune system healthy. Research suggests that drinking a couple of glasses of a concentrated cranberry juice drink every day may help to maintain a healthy urinary tract. It works by preventing bacteria from clinging to the walls of the bladder.

• Increase your child's intake of water. This will help to flush toxins and waste products from his system and prevent irritation of the urinary tract. Use a sports bottle so you can monitor how much he is drinking.

western herbalism

• Try a soothing barley water drink.

Simmer 100 g (about ¾ oz) rinsed barley in 600 ml (20 fl. oz) water until soft. Strain, then add a little lemon juice and honey to taste. Give as a lukewarm drink to your child several times a day.

• Goldenrod is anti-inflammatory, diuretic and antiseptic and it stimulates the immune system.

Make an infusion by adding 2 g (0.07 oz) of the plant to a cup of boiling water, leave to brew, then strain. Give your child 2 to 3 cups a day.

traditional chinese medicine

The kidneys are known as 'Fire at the Gate of Life' in Chinese medicine. Difficulty in urinating suggests a kidney or bladder disharmony, and frequent urination suggests a deficiency of kidney *chi*.

common sense

• Teach girls to wipe themselves from front to back after using the toilet.

• Dress your child in cotton underwear.

• Do not use bubble baths and talcum powder.

• Add a ½ teaspoonful of baking soda to a glass of water for your child to drink. This makes the urine more alkaline.

anxiety

You will soon know if your child is feeling anxious because she will start to breathe rapidly, perhaps panting and sighing. She may also visit the toilet more frequently or start complaining of headaches. Anxiety can make a child feel so unwell that you think there is something physically wrong with her. Handle your child sensitively and do not let her see that you are anxious about her anxiety.

common symptoms

- **Wheezing**
- **Coughing**
- **A sense of tightness in the chest, as if it is encased in a tight band**
- **Breathlessness that gets worse on contact with very cold air or when exercising**

complementary treatments

aromatherapy

Soothing essential oils include bergamot, mandarin, neroli, rose otto, Roman chamomile and frankincense. Add your chosen oil to a water spray and spritz into the room as required.

ayurvedic medicine

This is particularly helpful in treating stress-related disorders such as anxiety. You will be given advice about your child's lifestyle, such as diet, exercise and sleep, so that you can get the balance right, thus boosting her immunity and preventing illness. The practitioner may recommend yoga exercises and massage with a combination of oils and herbs to induce a sense of tranquillity. He may also suggest meditation techniques.

bach flower remedies

Rock Rose helps with fright, panic, terror and hysteria. Other remedies that help with anxiety include Beech, Chicory, Rock Water, Vervain and Vine. Rescue Remedy will also calm your child's emotions during a crisis.

arts therapies

These are especially beneficial for emotional and psychological disorders as they provide children with a means of expressing feelings that they often find too difficult to put into words.

yoga

If your child's mind is clear and focused she will be less likely to worry because she will not feel overwhelmed. Yoga focuses on breathing and posture, so oxygen will circulate properly to help her relax. Simple stretching techniques can really help with feelings of anxiety.

fears & phobias

Young children fear all sorts of things – the dark, animals, monsters, being left by their parents – and they have very powerful imaginations. Believing in monsters can be a way of giving shape to anxiety. In addition, once they go to school, they will face a whole new set of challenges, including pressure of schoolwork, peer pressure and even social rejection. Talk to your child about the situation as much as possible and provide plenty of opportunities for her to open up and discuss any problems.

symptoms

- **Stomach ache**
- **Headache**
- **Nausea and vomiting**
- **Crying**
- **Withdrawing into self**

complementary treatments

homeopathy

Argent nit can help your child to overcome nervousness and apprehension.

Lycopodium is the best remedy when your child is nervous and lacking in confidence about a particular situation.

Calc carb is indicated for children who find it hard to cope with change of routine.

traditional chinese medicine

Fear is a normal human emotion, but can lead to disharmony when it becomes chronic and the child cannot address the perceived cause of the fear. The organ most at risk is the kidneys, seen as the root of life and our will to succeed. Poor kidney function can lead to feelings of weakness and timidity, and physical symptoms such as night sweats and a dry mouth.

relaxation

Fear mobilizes the fight or flight mechanism, causing a huge surge of adrenaline. Your child's body will feel as if it is under attack, which has a knock-on effect on her immune system. Focus on the healing process of relaxation to boost her feelings of well-being. Get her to work around her body, tensing and releasing all the major muscle groups in turn.

arts therapies

These are especially beneficial for emotional and psychological disorders as they provide children with a means of expressing feelings that they often find too difficult to put into words. Many children naturally work through their fears with play. Encourage role play with favourite toys.

headaches

Children often complain of headaches and they can occur for a variety of reasons – and often for no reason at all! They are often a sign that a child is feeling under the weather, or has other symptoms that he cannot or does not want to talk about. Occasionally, headaches can indicate a more serious problem, such as raised blood pressure, a blow to the head or an infection.

common symptoms

- **Head pain, ranging from a mild ache to a deep throbbing pain**
- **Pain on one side of the head or all over**
- **Irritability, tiredness and crying**

Warning Call the doctor immediately if headache is accompanied by any of the following signs as they could indicate meningitis:

- Neck stiffness
- Drowsiness and difficulty in waking
- Vomiting or food refusal
- Fever
- Odd, staring expression
- Dislike of bright light
- Fretfulness and irritability
- Reddish-purple spots anywhere on the skin, which grow quickly into larger marks or bruises. Pressed under an empty glass, the spots don't go white, even for a few seconds.

triggers & irritants

- **Over-tiredness**
- **Stress, worry and excitement**
- **Colds, influenza, sinusitis and catarrh**
- **Ear ache**
- **Toothache**
- **Dehydration**
- **Eating the wrong foods**
- **Missing a meal**
- **Too much sun**
- **Getting over-heated**
- **Smoky atmospheres**
- **Watching too much TV or spending too long at a computer screen**

conventional treatment

Take your child's temperature and check for other symptoms. Give him some children's paracetamol and plenty of tender loving care. Consult your doctor if the headaches are frequent or particularly severe.

complementary treatments

aromatherapy

If you have a diffuser, add lavender, Roman chamomile and eucalyptus essential oils, and encourage your child to lie down and rest. Alternatively, make a soothing compress to apply to your child's head by soaking a clean cloth in water to which you have added a few drops of lavender and peppermint essential oils. Again, encourage your child to lie down in a darkened room.

homeopathy

Belladonna can be given for a pounding headache and those triggered by too much sun.

Gelsemium is indicated for headaches stemming from heavy congestion.

Mag phos can help with sharp pains that come and go.

kinesiology

This is effective in resolving everyday problems, such as headaches, which are troubling but not easy to cure. The practitioner will identify any allergies in order to stimulate the self-healing processes of your child's body and assess his muscle function in order to improve posture and body function.

nutritional therapy

If you suspect that your child's headaches are triggered by a food allergy, try an exclusion diet or allergy testing. Cheese and chocolate are two of the worst offenders.

traditional chinese medicine

Disharmony in the head area is very important in Chinese medicine, as the head is the confluence of all the yang channels. An excess of yang energy coming to the head can lead to problems such as headache and dizziness. Once any underlying imbalances have been addressed, the practitioner will prescribe herbs to treat the headache.

osteopathy

Some tension headaches are caused by skeletal problems and osteopathy helps by bringing the whole body back into balance in order to relieve the pain. Cranial osteopathy treatment is successful in dealing with symptoms resulting from direct trauma to the head – often the incident will have been forgotten yet headaches are the result.

chiropractic

Some tension headaches are triggered by physical problems, and chiropractors will treat headaches arising from problems in the neck area.

alexander technique

Poor posture and slumping can lead to headaches. This technique will re-educate your child's body so that he will learn to stand and move correctly and be more poised.

relaxation

If your child's headaches are triggered by stress or tension, try some simple relaxation techniques to help him relax.

common sense

• Dehydration is one of the most common causes of headaches. Make sure your child drinks enough, particularly on hot days and during sport.

• Encourage your child to lie down in a quiet, darkened room to help him relax.

• Fresh air will often help to clear a child's head.

• Don't let your child go for too long without food, as his blood sugar will drop, which can trigger headaches.

• Watch the weather – researchers in the USA have discovered that changes in the weather can trigger headaches.

stress

When children are upset or over-excited, their nervous system reacts by releasing a rush of adrenaline, and energy flows away from the digestive system. This often leads to the nagging aches and upset stomachs that are characteristic of stress. It can be a normal part of everyday life for many children, and the important thing is to learn how to control it.

common symptoms

- Upset stomach with cramps and spasms
- Headaches
- Constipation/diarrhoea
- Irritability
- Loss of sense of humour
- Poor concentration
- Feeling defensive
- Insomnia
- Sweating
- Breathlessness
- Loss of appetite/binge eating
- Eczema
- Asthma

triggers & irritants

- School work
- Emotional problems
- Peer pressure
- Difficulties at home
- Feelings of being unable to cope
- Feelings of being out of control

conventional treatment

There is no specific treatment, but if your child regularly exhibits symptoms of stress, consult your doctor.

complementary treatments

aromatherapy

The following essential oils are relaxing and comforting: lavender, petitgrain, Roman chamomile and ylang-ylang. Add your chosen oil to a water spray and spritz into your child's room as required.

western herbalism

Herbs that support the nervous system, helping the child to relax and reducing stress and tension, include chamomile, peppermint and lemon balm. They are also excellent remedies for settling an upset stomach.

bach flower remedies

Rescue Remedy will help your child to cope in an emergency. It comprises Impatiens (for agitation accompanying stress), Clematis (for disorientation accompanying trauma), Rock Rose (for panic and fright) and Cherry Plum (for fear of losing control). Add 4 drops to a small glass of water and get your child to sip this mixture as necessary.

relaxation

Visualization is one of the most useful ways of increasing the benefits of relaxation. Encourage your child to use her imagination by asking her to think about a special place, such as the beach on holiday. This can help to induce a calm and relaxed state.

reflexology

Reflexology helps to alleviate the effects of stress by inducing deep relaxation, allowing the nervous system to function and rebalancing the body. Parents can use it to ease the stress in their child's everyday life.

This use of touch will help you to build a healthy caring relationship with your child, who will gain a sense of worth and well-being from knowing you are paying them special attention. Using reflexology techniques for relaxation helps the body to break up and interrupt particular patterns of stress, so that it does not build up and cause wear and tear on the body.

Reflexology can also help you to gain a better picture of your child's health. For example, you may think that your child is faking a stomach ache to get out of going to school, but if she says 'ouch' when you press the stomach reflex point of her foot, you will know that it is a genuine complaint.

alexander technique

This can help with stress-related psychosomatic conditions. By re-educating your child's body to be more co-ordinated the technique will teach her to gradually let go of tension.

yoga

Learning to breathe correctly will enhance your child's capacity to stay calm and relaxed in stressful situations.

arts therapies

These are especially beneficial for emotional and psychological disorders as they provide children with a non-verbal means of expressing their feelings.

common sense

Give your child extra love, support and reassurance to help her through stressful times and emotional upsets.

hyperactivity

Hyperactivity is an increasing problem, and attention deficit and hyperactivity disorder (ADHD) is one of the fastest growing conditions among children, particularly boys. If your child is demanding, has a poor attention span, appears to need little sleep and exhibits aggressive behaviour, he may have ADHD. While many parents refer to their children as hyperactive, in reality they are often little more than simply boisterous.

common symptoms

- Restlessness
- Over-talkative
- Over-excitability
- Constant fidgeting or changing activities
- Poor sleep patterns/constant waking in the night
- Violent temper tantrums

triggers & irritants

- Food intolerance
- Vitamin or mineral deficiencies
- Family history of asthma, eczema and hay fever
- Pollution – inhaling toxic metals can affect brain function

conventional treatment

If you feel your child has some or all of the symptoms of ADHD, consult your doctor. The stimulant drug Ritalin is frequently prescribed, but it has a number of side-effects and does not address the underlying issues, such as food intolerance.

complementary treatments

aromatherapy

• Essential oils can be wonderfully calming. Try diluting mandarin, lavender and Roman chamomile in vegetable oil and adding to your child's bathwater.

• Studies show that essential oils can also help with concentration. Try diffusing one of the stimulating oils, such as lemon, bergamot, grapefruit or pine, into the atmosphere to help your child focus.

osteopathy

Cranial osteopathy can help with restlessness and hyperactive behaviour. Careful examination can reveal distortions, sometimes going back to birth itself, which can interfere with the development of the nervous system.

bach flower remedies

• Vervain is used for those who are over-enthusiastic and over-powering, so is helpful for children who cannot relax.

• Impatiens is useful for those who act quickly and are impatient and irritable.

nutritional therapy

Hyperactivity is often related to food intolerance, particularly to sugar and refined carbohydrates, food colourings and flavourings. Nutritional deficiencies can affect brain function, so check he is getting the recommended amounts of iron, zinc, B vitamins and magnesium.

sleep problems

Children often develop sleep problems as they grow up, even if they were able to drop off straight away when they were younger. Hyperactive children have great difficulty getting to sleep and tend to wake again after a few hours. Establish a bedtime routine with clear boundaries that are non-negotiable. Get your child into the habit of winding down before bedtime by having a quiet rest and relaxation period.

triggers & irritants

- An over-active mind
- Anxiety and stress
- Major life changes, such as new baby or starting school
- Over-tiredness
- Lack of fresh air or exercise
- Breathing conditions, such as asthma and catarrh
- Nightmares
- Fear of the dark

conventional treatment

There is no specific treatment but, if your child regularly has problems getting to sleep, discuss it with your doctor.

complementary treatments

homeopathy

Argent nit can work wonders if your child is anxious about a particular event.

Coffea is helpful for children who cannot sleep because they are over-excited.

nutritional therapy

Make sure your child is eating well and avoid junk food, especially sugar. Remember that cola drinks and cocoa contain caffeine, which affects the brain and nervous system and can affect sleep. Do not let your child eat just before bedtime.

traditional chinese medicine

Sleep and energy patterns are indications of the health of the *chi*, blood and the yin of the body. Difficulty in getting to sleep points to a blood deficiency, continually waking suggests a kidney disharmony and disturbed dreams suggests a liver or heart disharmony.

yoga

Gentle yoga exercises will help your child to get a good night's sleep, freeing tension from his mind and body. It is an ideal way of winding down after a busy day.

relaxation

Add a few drops of lavender essential oil mixed in a teaspoonful of vegetable oil to a warm bath before bedtime. Offer your child a cup of chamomile or lemon balm herbal tea sweetened with honey. Ask him to lie down and do some relaxation exercises.

index

acknowledgements

Executive editor: Jane McIntosh

Editor: Emma Pattison

Executive art editor: Rozelle Bentheim

Designer: Geoff Borin

Illustrator: Nicola Gregory

Production controller: Ian Paton